*Anne Marie has prepared excellent guided meditations for
many self-discovery purposes: therapy, group workshops and retreats,
and for one's own creative inspiration. I love the book's simple and concise
advice on how to lead a guided meditation. Anne Marie offers good
preparation for those who are new to facilitating these journeys.
Magical Inner Journeys is a mini-library available to new
or experienced facilitators looking for guided meditations.*

~ Kylea Taylor, author of The Ethics of Caring

*Anne Marie weaves a gentle wondrous journey in these scripts.
I love her imagery, and what a powerful set up for SoulCollage®.
I will use these again and again!*

~ Jennifer Louden, Author, JenniferLouden.com

*Wonderfully imaginative! Anne Marie's
Magical Inner Journeys invite deep experiences
and unearth truly magical wisdom.*

~ Jill Badonsky, Author, KaizenMuse.com

*These special inner journeys open doors
that allow new and surprising ways of meeting our inner parts.
In each, we are brought gently and slowly to a state of wonderful
relaxation in readiness for the visualization of
the members of our inner "committee."*

~ Imelda Maguire, SoulCollage® Facilitator, Ireland

44 GUIDED IMAGERY SCRIPTS TO INSPIRE SELF-DISCOVERY WITH SOULCOLLAGE®

ANNE MARIE BENNETT

Magical Inner Journeys

44 Guided Imagery
Scripts to Inspire
Self-Discovery
with SoulCollage®

ANNE MARIE BENNETT

Copyright © 2018 Anne Marie Bennett
All rights reserved.

Please do not copy, forward, give away or reproduce this
material in any manner without written permission from the author.

Many hours and much creative energy were devoted to the creation of this book.
Your purchase supports the continuing efforts of KaleidoSoul.com in its mission
to make SoulCollage® available to people around the world.
To give feedback or to contact the author, please email:
annemarie@kaleidosoul.com.

**SoulCollage® is a trademarked process,
created by Seena Frost.**

Cover design and book design by Carol Coogan.
To contact please email: info@carolcoogandesign.com.
www.carolcoogandesign.com

All rights reserved.
ISBN: 1985502216
ISBN-13: 978-1985502215

Published by KaleidoSoul Media, PO Box 745, Beverly MA 01915

Dedication

For all those who have allowed me
to lead them on these Magical Inner Journeys
as part of my SoulCollage® workshops
and retreats, online and in person.

And for SoulCollage® Facilitators everywhere.

As Seena Frost once said,
"You are all my seeds, spreading many seeds all over."

May these guided imagery scripts help you to continue
to spread the seeds of SoulCollage®, creativity, and
inner awakenings all over our wide, wide world

Contents

Introduction 2
How to Use This Book 4
Part 1 **Inner Treasures** 9
    Journey with a SoulCollage® Card 10
    Inner Sanctuary 12
    Inner Garden 14
    Treasure Chest 18
    Inner Guidance System (Your IGS) 20
    Walking Your Internal Red Carpet 22
    Opening to Blossom 24
    Breaking Into Flower 26
    The Puzzle of Your Life – Part 1 28
    The Puzzle of Your Life - Part 2 30

Part 2 **Be Here Now** 33
    Be Here Now 34
    Velvet Blanket 38
    Lotus Flower of Self-Blessing 40
    Touching Peace 42
    The Mirror 44
    Light Up Your Holidays 48
    Lucky Leprechaun 50
    Table of Creativity 52

Part 3 **Inner Voices** 55
    Magic Bus Ride 56
    The Conference Table 59
    Dancing with Your Inner Child 62
    Inner Queen 66
    O Come All Ye Playful 68
    Taking the Inner Critic Out of the Director's Chair ... 70
    The Great White Feather 74
    Offering Comfort to a Hurting Committee Part 76

Part 4 Community 79
    Indra's Net 80
    Blessed Community Circle 82
    Loving-Kindness (Metta) 84

Part 5 Archetypes 87
    Meeting a Council Guide 88
    Meeting Your Creative Muse 90
    Archetypes Along Your Journey 94
    Council Circle 98
    Butterfly Woman 1 100
    Butterfly Woman 2 102

Part 6 Animal Companions 105
    Meeting an Animal Guide 106
    Sacred Animals Circle 108

Part 7 Spirituality 115
    Circled on a Map 116
    Plugging Into Source 118
    Journey to the Center of You 121

Part 8 Miscellaneous 125
    Yellow Brick Road- Part 1 126
    Yellow Brick Road- Part 2 128
    Gaining Perspective 131

Gratitudes 136
Resources 138

… Isn't it splendid to think of all the things there are to find out about? It just makes me feel glad to be alive—it's such an interesting world. It wouldn't be half so interesting if we knew all about everything, would it? There'd be no scope for imagination then, would there?

~ L.M. Montgomery

Magical Inner Journeys

44 Guided Imagery Scripts to Inspire Self-Discovery with SoulCollage®

Introduction

I have fallen in love with the imagination. And if you fall in love with the imagination, you understand that it is a free spirit. It will go anywhere, and it can do anything.

~ Alice Walker

My first guided imagery experience was in 1969. I was 13 years old, lying on the hard floor of our middle school gymnasium. Our P.E. teacher (sorry, I can't remember her name) asked us to close our eyes. I remember that it was the middle of winter, bitter cold outside. But here… in our imaginations, she was leading us to a warm, sunny meadow. I could see it. I could feel it. I wasn't in wintry New England anymore. I was somewhere else entirely and I hadn't even left the building! The fact that I could close my eyes and picture myself somewhere else so easily. . . well, it was extraordinary.

I don't remember the rest of the journey our teacher took us on that day. Heck, I don't even remember why she did it in the first place! And I don't recall it ever happening again while I was in school. But that experience has always stayed with me as the first time I purposely used my imagination to take an "inner journey."

In my twenties, I was teaching second grade in a small country town in Virginia. I found a cassette tape (yes, well, that was the 80's) of guided meditations for children and was thrilled to discover that they loved them as much as I did. Pretty soon I was making up my own stories and turning them into short "inner journeys" for my students.

Later on my life journey I discovered a recording of guided meditations by Alan Cohen, and listening to them pretty much saved my life during a very difficult time in my late twenties and early thirties. From then on, I was hooked. I found that guided imagery allowed me to "go within" and explore my inner landscape; it helped me to transform areas of darkness into light, despair into hope, and confusion into peace. It was also a blessing because it encouraged me to stay connected to myself and to Spirit when those connections were lacking in my life.

During the period of time when I was first discovering and using SoulCollage®, I was also healing from a year of breast cancer surgeries and treatments. A wonderful therapist named Fran accompanied me on this healing journey, and she guided me through many "inner journeys" during our sessions together. Many of those guided journeys precipitated new SoulCollage® cards. I was learning the language of my inner world, meeting my inner committee voices, gaining wisdom from archetypal spirit guides and animal companions. The blend of my own SoulCollage® play with the imagery work that I did with Fran made a huge difference in how my body, mind, and spirit healed from the cancer, and how I was able to transform my life into one where I was following my heart and passion instead of "doing" my life the way I'd always done it.

When I began facilitating SoulCollage® in 2005, I realized what a perfect complement guided imagery would be to my workshops. The very first one I wrote was "Indra's Net." I was leading a workshop on the Community Suit and wanted a way for the participants to really grasp the concept that we are *all* connected. The guided imagery script included in this book is what came forth.

I want you to know that I don't use the phrase "came forth" lightly. It is an accurate description of how these scripts have come into being. Yes, each one started with my idea. And yes, it's true, I sat down at my laptop and "wrote" each one. However, the experience of bringing these guided imageries forth has been very different from other kinds of writing that I have done over the years. Spirit has definitely shaped and formed these scripts.

I have found that when I sit down to "write" a guided imagery script, a mysterious, almost magical Something Else takes over. I once heard Mark Nepo say of his own writing, "I push the pen until it pulls me," and that is the exact experience I have when one of these scripts is coming forth. I start the process by pushing my pen (or in my case, my fingers on the laptop) with an idea and a few words . . . and then I am pulled by something greater; the words simply flow, and what results is a Magical Inner Journey.

Someone once asked me why I call my guided imageries "Magical Inner Journeys." They are MAGICAL because they invite you to use your imagination in a gentle, authentic way. Because of this, transformation can begin, which often feels like magic. They are also magical because anything can happen once you begin! The magic is limited only by your imagination. Each of these scripts is designed to take you INWARD, to the depths of your being, however deep you are willing and able to go. Also, each one takes you on an inner JOURNEY that has a beginning, a middle, and an end. On this journey, you'll discover parts of yourself perhaps long forgotten, gifts long neglected, and inner landscapes unexplored.

It is with great excitement and joy that I offer these Magical Inner Journey scripts to the world at large. My hope is that they will deepen your own relationship with yourself, with others, and with Spirit, however you choose to call Spirit.

Whether you use them in written form on your own to dive deeper within yourself using your imagination, or you use them as a SoulCollage® Facilitator to help participants understand themselves and the process more fully . . . it doesn't matter. What matters always is the journey itself.

I wish you peace, joy, and many blessings along the way.

Anne Marie Bennett
April 2018
Beverly, Massachusetts

How to Use This Book

Please read this whole section carefully before using any of the guided imagery scripts in this book!

For Personal Use

You will find these scripts easy to use on your own
for your personal and/or spiritual growth.

Here are some suggestions:

1. Scan through the book and find a script that seems to be calling to your heart. You don't need to know why.

2. Read the script all the way through once or twice.

3. Find a comfortable place to sit or lie down. Eliminate distractions, such as the phone, and ensure that you won't be interrupted.

4. Close your eyes and enter the journey as you remember it from the script. It's perfectly okay if the story veers off into new territory. Make it your own!

5. Another option is to record the script in your own voice, or ask someone else to record it for you. Then follow step #3, close your eyes and listen to the recording.

6. When the journey is complete, be sure to bring yourself back slowly and gently. Give yourself at least five minutes to either sit in silence, absorbing the experience into your being, or to journal about it. If journaling doesn't feel satisfying, try finding a different way to process and express what happened for you on the inner journey. Some examples: create a collage, create a SoulCollage® card, watercolor, dance, sing or write a song, move into some yoga postures, paint or draw.

7. Many of the scripts in this book are available as recordings in MP3 download or CD format. You'll find more information at www.KaleidoSoul.com/cds and www.KaleidoSoul.com/oasis

For Facilitators

First of all, honor yourself for purchasing this book!
I trust that it will serve you and your workshop participants for many years to come.

Many Facilitators I know (including me!) have used one or more of these scripts as the basis for a whole workshop or weekend retreat. You'll find several guided imageries here for each of the suits. There are a few guided imageries that relate to the Transpersonal cards in the Spirituality section. There are also many scripts that don't particularly fit into any one suit, but they can easily be worked into an Introduction to SoulCollage® workshop, or any other themed class that you might be presenting.

Here are my best suggestions for integrating these
guided imagery experiences into a workshop setting:

1. Read through all of the scripts first and allow your own creativity to be inspired.

2. Choose one and guide yourself through the Magical Inner Journey. Find a comfortable place to sit or lie down. Eliminate distractions such as the phone, and ensure that you won't be interrupted.

3. Close your eyes and enter the journey as you remember it from the script. It's perfectly okay if the story veers off into new territory. Make it your own!

4. When the journey is complete, be sure to bring yourself back slowly and gently. Give yourself at least five minutes to either sit in silence, absorbing the experience into your being, or to journal about it. If journaling doesn't feel satisfying, try finding a different way to process and express what happened for you on the inner journey. Some examples: create a collage, create a SoulCollage® card, watercolor, dance, sing or write a song, move into some yoga postures, paint or draw.

5. Then flip on your Facilitator cap and make some notes about how you could use this script in a workshop setting. How might you introduce it? What might you invite participants to do afterwards?

6. Just as you trust the SoulCollage® process, I invite you to trust your own inner guidance . . . always and in all ways!

7. Many of the scripts in this book are available as recordings in MP3 download or CD format. You'll find more information at www.KaleidoSoul.com/cds and www.KaleidoSoul.com/oasis.

8. Please email me anytime if you have a question about a particular script, or would like guidance about how to use it within a SoulCollage® workshop or retreat setting.

Tips for Reading Scripts Aloud

Introducing the Magical Inner Journey

It is important to always preface any guided imagery experience by giving participants permission to make the inner journey their own.

Here's an example of what I always say before beginning to lead any guided imagery:

> *In this Magical Inner Journey, I'm going to be inviting you to see things in your imagination. But not everyone sees things; not everyone is visual. If you're more auditory, you might be more aware of hearing sounds or words. Kinesthetic people sometimes simply explore their inner landscape by the sense of touch. Some people just have an idea about what is happening on the inner journey. And then again, some people feel so relaxed and comfortable that they fall asleep! I always say that everyone gets exactly what they need from these guided journeys, so just allow your experience to be just what it is. Give yourself permission to get what you need from this time of relaxation. I will be guiding you through the whole inner journey, and you can open your eyes at any time if you need to come back before I'm done. It's all okay!*

I strongly suggest that you preface each of these scripts with a similar invitation.

Even though it takes a minute or two, it is important because it embraces what we stress during our SoulCollage® Facilitator Trainings, which is that people coming to our workshops are seeking three things: protection, permission, and connection. This concept is written about more fully by Kylea Taylor in her book, The Ethics of Caring. It resulted from the collaboration of Kylea and two other Holotropic Breathwork® Facilitators as they were designing a module for the Grof Transpersonal Training in 2000. Its application is broad and pertinent to many different healing modalities. Let's look at it here in relation to choosing to use guided imagery in our SoulCollage® workshops:

> **Protection** — People need to know that they are safe. When they hear you share the above paragraph before the guided imagery begins, they will be able to relax a bit more, knowing that you are guiding the journey. They will also feel safe because you've given them permission to do whatever they need to do to take care of themselves throughout the inner journey. Safety also ensues within each guided imagery script as participants are given choices.

> **Permission** — People need permission to be able to make the process their own. They need to know that there's no way to do it "right," and that no one is going to judge them, no matter what they do or say (even if they fall asleep!).

> **Connection** — People need to feel a sense of connection with themselves, with others, and with Spirit (however they define Spirit). Prefacing a guided imagery with the above paragraph gives your workshop participants a sense of connection with you, and helps them to relax enough so that they can perhaps connect with others about the experience after the inner journey is complete.

Also, if you are going to ask them to journal when the imagery is over, you will want to make sure that everyone has a pen and paper nearby before you begin. This allows the transition to be much smoother when you are finished with the script.

During the Magical Inner Journey

Here are my best suggestions for the time when you are reading the script aloud and guiding everyone through the journey:

1. Read slowly. Read even slower than you think you should be reading!

2. Practice reading the script aloud before the workshop.

3. Pause often! In the scripts, a pause is indicated every time you see: …
   Each new paragraph indicates a longer pause as well.

4. Find your own rhythm. Make the script your own, keeping the cardinal rule of "Read slowly" always in mind.

5. You have my permission to adapt/adjust the script for your audience in any way that you need to.

6. Follow your own intuition as you lead the inner journey. Change wording if needed, to make it more personal for your audience.

7. Be aware of your participants as you guide the journey. Be sure you have a few boxes of tissues available if needed. If someone begins snoring loudly, you may add a line such as, "Keep focusing on my words… allow any sounds in the environment to blend right in to your experience…" Don't worry if you notice that someone's eyes are open. They are choosing to experience the guided imagery that way, and it's all okay.

8. **Keep in mind that these Magical Inner Journeys are not meant to stand alone. It is important to preface the journey (see above) as well as offer some follow-up activity to help participants integrate the journey into their life (see below).**

After the Magical Inner Journey

**What happens when you've read the last word of the script?
Believe me when I say that the journey isn't over!**

It is vitally important that participants have some way to process the experience, either within themselves, or out loud. Keep in mind the needs of your audience as you choose exactly how to bring closure to each Magical Inner Journey experience.

Here are some suggestions for follow-up activities:

1. Invite participants to spend five-ten minutes journaling (or drawing) on their own about the experience. You might remind them orally of the key points of the journey, to refresh their memories. For example, after the "Inner Garden" journey, you might suggest, "What did your garden look like? What kind of flower was at the center? What did your flower say to you?"

2. If you are inviting them to journal for several minutes, also offer them the option of not journaling so they can soak in the silence and allow the imagery to settle within them. Some people prefer that to immediately writing about the experience.

3. Once participants have had a chance to process the inner journey alone in their journal, you could divide participants into pairs or triads, and invite them to share as much or as little as they choose about what happened for them during the journey. Trust your intuition about whether this is a viable option for your participants. For some, it will be enough to journal on their own.

4. Always allow time for a couple of people to speak their experience aloud to the whole group. Some people need to process orally instead of, or in addition to, processing in writing. Be aware of the time. In order to avoid someone taking over and going on and on (and on!), I usually say something like, "We have time for two or three people to share briefly about their inner journey." Including this sharing is a good way to bring everyone back together into the larger group (more connection!).

5. Remind everyone that you will be available during card making time if anyone would like to share their inner journey experience with you privately.

6. Once you have allowed people time to process their individual journeys through writing, and out loud, it's time to invite card making! At this point it's a good idea to take a few minutes to share some of your own cards on the particular theme of the Magical Inner Journey you were leading.

7. After card making, it is important to always bring participants back together for a journaling activity where they can tune in to the energy of one of the cards they made. For more ideas on journaling with a SoulCollage® card, please visit www.KaleidoSoul.com/soulcollage-cards-interpreting

8. Please share with me any other follow-up activities that you try with these scripts, and I will include them in a future edition of this book. My email is: kaleidosoul@gmail.com.

Part 1

Inner Treasures

Imagination is more important than knowledge. Knowledge is limited. Imagination encircles the world.

~ Albert Einstein

Journey with a SoulCollage® Card

Before we begin this journey, please place one of your SoulCollage® cards in front of you. If you don't have any SoulCollage® cards yet, you can use an image from a magazine that intrigues you. You can do this same meditation many, many times and use a different card each time. Or use the same card several weeks in a row and see how deep you can go with it.

Please take a moment to move your body into a comfortable position. I invite you now to take a moment to gaze at your SoulCollage® card or your magazine image… Slowly scan it from top to bottom… and from side to side… Taking note of the setting… Taking note of each being or object that is on the card…. If you have already done some work with this card… just try setting that aside for a moment and looking at it anew…

If you like, use one finger to trace around the edge of the card slowly… noticing anything about the edges or border of the card or image… And then try tracing around any of the figures or objects that are there as well…

When you are ready, allow your eyes to softly close… and bring your whole self to a sweet centered stillness… Giving yourself permission to relax… Taking time out of your busy day to pause… and pay attention to your breath… Just noticing as you breathe in… and as you breathe out… Breathing in the stillness that is always inside of you… Breathing out any inner chaos… Breathing in a radical acceptance… an acceptance that embraces and encompasses all parts of you… And then breathing out any thoughts that get in the way of that acceptance… Giving yourself permission to just breathe in… to just breathe out… and to simply relax…

Now in your imagination… if you choose… enter the setting of your SoulCollage® card… Join the being or beings that are on this card…Notice what happens when you connect with these images…. Just spend a few moments in silence with this energy… Remember, this is your inner journey… You are safe and protected at all times…

Breathing in and out now… with the energy of this card or image…

If you choose to, go ahead and ask this being "Who are you?"
and listen as it responds… What is its story?...

You might also want to ask "What do you need from me?"…

or "What special message do you have for me today?"… Allow this being time to answer you… and then listen… just listen… Remaining as open as you can to the possibility of any answers you are given…

Now, taking a moment to find a way to thank this being, this image… knowing that you can come back and spend time with it whenever you like… Knowing also that you can choose to bring its energy back with you into the world in some special way…

I invite you now to think about returning from your inner journey… I invite you to focus on your breath now… Sensing all the parts of your body against your chair or the floor… Following the sound of my voice back to this present moment… If it feels good to do so, you might want to stretch your arms and legs a little, or maybe move your head slowly from side to side… And in whatever way feels good to you, accompanying yourself back into your body… If you choose to do so, try offering a prayer of thanksgiving for the gift of your imagination and for this particular SoulCollage® card (or image) and its message for you today…

Allowing your eyes to open when you are ready… Taking your time…
I will wait for you… All is well…

Inner Sanctuary

Begin by making yourself comfortable wherever you are right now…
Please listen to your body and respect whatever it is asking you for in this moment…

I invite you to close your eyes whenever you feel ready to do so… And now try focusing on your breath for a moment… Feel the air flowing in and out of your nostrils… in… and out… in… and out… Feel your chest rising and falling with each breath… rising and falling… rising and falling… rising and falling…

Now you are feeling very comfortable and more relaxed… In your imagination I invite you to see a path… It can be any kind of a path… a little trail in the woods… a country road… a brick walkway in a garden… This path can be anywhere you want it to be… by the ocean… in the city… up a mountain… in a meadow…

Wherever this path is… know that it is a path created just for you… It is a friendly path… You feel safe on this path… And as you start walking on this path, you feel a lovely sense of expectancy and joy…

Continuing to walk on this special path that is your own…
Following it and trusting that it will lead you where you need to go today…

As you walk… you are looking around you… observing… What do you see?… What colors surround you?… What sounds do you hear as you continue to walk on your path?… You are just listening… What can you smell?…

As you continue on this path, after a while, you are going to come upon your very own sanctuary… This inner sanctuary is a safe place in your imagination that you can access any time you need it for shelter… for comfort… for support…

Continuing to explore your particular inner path now… And when you see your inner sanctuary space up ahead… I invite you to stop walking for a moment… and just stand still in front of it for a little while… Your sanctuary space can be any kind of a structure that you choose… This is your path and it's your sanctuary… It might look like a house… or a cottage… It might be a castle… or a large tent… a barn… a cave… a treehouse… Make it exactly what feels right to you… Make it a very special place that you will want to come back to again and again…

So you are simply standing in front of your inner sanctuary now… Noticing as much as you can about it… What color or colors is it?… What is all around it?…

Remember, this is a completely safe place for you…
This is an inner refuge and a place of joyful discovery…

If you choose to, go ahead and walk up to the main entrance of your sanctuary…
If it feels good to you, you can enter… And now you are just taking a few minutes to explore… Allowing the music to carry you as you investigate your inner sanctuary for a few minutes on your own…. Walking around… Seeing what there is to see… Remember, this is your own inner creation… This sanctuary space is totally safe and secure… The only surprises you will find here are good ones…

It's almost time to leave your sanctuary for now… Remember, you can always come back here… anytime you want… just by closing your eyes and taking a breath…

I invite you now to find your way back to the door or entrance that you came in… And next to that entrance is a small table… And on that table is a blue velvet box… In the box there is a gift for you… just for you…

So now you are opening the blue velvet box… and taking out the gift that is there for you… Examining it… admiring it… Opening your heart to receive this gift… this very special gift…

It's time to think about leaving for now… Be sure to bring the gift back with you… It's important that you don't leave it behind… Carrying the gift however you need to… and now exiting your inner sanctuary the same way you entered…

Following the path that led you here… Following it back… and back… and back… until you are once again able to feel your body resting on your chair…

And now bringing yourself back to your breath… Noticing the breath as it enters through your nose and mouth on an inhale… Noticing how it shimmers through your whole body, then exits as you exhale… Feeling your stomach and chest rising and falling with each breath…

Begin to pay attention to your body again… your feet… legs… stomach… chest…. arms… shoulders… neck… head… You might want to lightly flex your fingers and toes… or gently shake out your arms and legs…

When you are ready… and only when you are ready… open your eyes… Take your time… I will wait for you… Grounding yourself back in this present moment… Remembering that all is well.

Inner Garden

I invite you now to take a deep breath and allow your eyes to close…
Giving your body permission to relax and be comfortable…
as comfortable as you can be in this moment…

As much as you can, allow your body to experience the contact that it makes with the chair and with the floor… and let your body adjust itself in any way it needs… in order to be fully comfortable… Listening to your body… Adjusting as necessary…

As you tune in to the rhythm of your breathing, imagine that when you inhale… you're inhaling a little bit of the sky… and it's very clear and very refreshing… And as you exhale, imagine that you're letting go of whatever you don't need right now… Inhaling the light, clear sky… Exhaling that which does not serve you right now…

Letting the rhythm of your breath be just what it is… a simple and beautiful process of taking in what's fresh and clear… and letting go of what's no longer needed…

Each breath you take relaxes and refreshes you… Your breathing and your mind are becoming clearer and clearer… Your body is relaxing a little bit more with each inhale and exhale…

Allowing your imagination to be open and receptive… Breathing in… and breathing out… You're going to take a little journey now… a magical journey to the very center of your being… to your inner world… to the deepest, most authentic part of you… Let's go there now….

I invite you to use your imagination to picture yourself sitting in a cozy little movie theatre… If you don't like movie theatres, you could imagine yourself in another kind of theatre… or just a room with a screen on the front wall… It is dark and quiet here… You are sitting alone, wondering what the movie will be about… Maybe you are munching on popcorn… Maybe you're simply curious, sitting still and waiting for this movie…

Now the screen is lighting up… and on the screen you are seeing a garden… a beautiful garden… You are watching carefully as the camera pans all the way around this amazing garden… You are beginning to sense that this garden is familiar to you somehow… You are recognizing this garden… because it is a part of you and always has been… This is your very own inner garden…

You are brimming with curiosity now… So you find yourself standing up and walking to the screen… You are reaching your hand out and to your amazement, you find that you are drawn right into the screen… into the picture that is in front of you… into this beautiful inner garden…

You are standing on the edge of the garden now… If you choose, go ahead and take a few minutes to explore this garden fully… from one end to the other… simply observing… What season is it?... How does the air feel?... What's the weather like in your garden?... What is growing here?... Is this garden well-tended… or does it need some weeding… some pruning?... How does the soil feel when you bend down and sift some through your fingers?... Does it need water… or more sun… or is it just right?...

Continuing to explore your inner garden now… Simply noticing, without judgment… Simply being aware of what is around you… Are there well-marked paths or is it hard to find your way around?... What sounds are you hearing as you walk through your garden?... Are there any smells in the air that you especially love?…
Continuing to explore for a few minutes now…
Exploring this inner garden that is yours and yours alone…

And now, wherever you are in your garden, I invite you to find your way to the center… to the center of your beautiful inner garden… And in the center of your garden, you find the most beautiful flower you've ever seen… the most beautiful flower…
If you like, walk up to this flower now and sit down next to it… What kind of a flower is growing here?... Is it a flower that you recognize or is it a flower you've never seen before?... What color or colors is it?... If you choose to, take a moment to lean towards it and smell it… What does it smell like?... Gently and reverently touch its petals if you like… How do they feel to your fingers?... Taking some time to notice anything else about this flower…

As you are sitting with the flower, you are realizing that it is magical… It represents your soul… It knows exactly who you are… And it has all the wisdom in the universe stored in its very essence… It has all the answers to all of your questions right there written into its beauty… because it is a part you… and it has been with you on your entire life's journey…

If it feels right, I invite you to lean a little closer to your flower and let it whisper a special secret in your ear… a secret meant for you and you alone…

Or perhaps you've been struggling with a question or an issue in your life…
If so, you might want to let your flower whisper an answer to you… Listen…
What is it telling you?… What has it been trying to say to you for a long time?…

So now it's almost time to say good-bye to your flower… And you are remembering
that you can come back here any time you want to… This inner garden is a special
place of retreat and comfort that you can come to any time you wish…

And now finding a way to say good-bye to your flower… Knowing that it
is right here for you any time you need its wisdom…its comfort… its beauty…

You are walking back through your garden now… enjoying every breath
you are taking in this magical inner garden that is your growing place…

Finding the place where you stepped into the garden… and then stepping…
carefully… back out… back into the darkened movie theatre…

And now finding your seat in the theatre… Sitting quietly as you allow this experience
to be absorbed into your senses… your breath… your body… your being…

Feeling your legs and back against the chair that you are sitting on in this room
today… And finding your way back to the sound of my voice… Feeling both of your
feet planted firmly on the floor… Allowing yourself to breathe a little deeper now…
And coming back to all the sensations of your body…

And when you're ready… go ahead and open your eyes… grounding yourself
in the presence of everyone here… taking your time… I will wait for you…
And remembering that all is well…

Treasure Chest

Please sit as comfortably as you can in your chair with your feet flat on the floor to ground you… Sitting up straight and tall… Straight spine… Breathing deeply as you allow yourself to settle into yourself right now… in this moment… Surrendering your body into the safety of the chair that is supporting you… And closing your eyes when you are ready… or keeping a soft gaze downward if that feels more comfortable to you…

Taking a deep breath in… and letting it go… Taking another deep breath… and letting it go… And now one more deep breath… and letting it go…

Inviting your body to relax just a little bit more with each breath… Inhaling relaxation… and then exhaling any tension that might be making its home in your body or mind… Inhaling relaxation…and exhaling tension… Allowing yourself to be more and more centered… and more and more relaxed…

Now… in your imagination… find yourself in your inner sanctuary space… a place or building that has been created just for you and your inner explorations… Knowing in your very depths that this is a safe and completely secure place for you to go within… And now just walking around for a bit… just exploring… and noticing anything that you see… hear… smell… feel… Noticing how your body feels… Are you moving slowly?… Or maybe you feel like skipping or hopping or dancing… There is no right or wrong way… and you are just moving around your private sanctuary space… however you feel led to move…

I invite you now to stop for a moment and look all around you… Find your favorite place in your inner sanctuary space… Just looking all around until you find a place that seems to be inviting you… And if you choose to, go ahead and go there now… sitting down… relaxing… breathing…

As you are looking around this new setting… you notice that there is a large box right next to you… It looks like a treasure chest… Hmmm… Just looking at it for a moment… Noticing what it's made of… Noticing its color… its shape… Then picking it up and holding it in your lap… What does it feel like in your hands?… Can you sense any curiosity about what might be inside?…

Inside this treasure chest there will be many gifts, many treasures that await you… This treasure chest holds all the bright and lovely parts of yourself… all the parts of yourself that you really like… the parts that others admire and cherish about you…

I'm inviting you now… if it feels right… to open the treasure chest that is on your lap… and see what is inside just for you… Sifting through these gifts… these treasures… these bright and beautiful symbols of your best, most authentic qualities…
What are you finding here?... Maybe there is compassion… love… creativity… power… blessings… happy memories… What else are you finding here?...

Not trying to make anything happen… just letting these treasures show themselves to you… If you are opening the treasure chest and it appears empty for now, allow that to be okay too… Your particular treasures will make themselves known to you in a different way or at a different time… Knowing that it's all good… whatever is happening … And it's all okay…

In just a moment I'm going to invite you to do one of two things… You can either close the box and set it back on the ground beside you… Or you can put your hands out in front of you… and imagine the treasure chest shrinking… shrinking small enough to fit in the palm of your hand… and then imagine opening your heart and putting the chest inside your heart for safe-keeping…

So go ahead and do one of those things right now… Set the chest on the ground… or shrink it to fit in your palm… and then place it gently in your heart…

Now, slowly standing up… still in your imagination… Stretching and breathing deeply in this wondrous space… Then beginning to walk back to the place where you entered your inner sanctuary…

And as you step out of this sacred space… if it feels right… find yourself turning around and making a little bow to it… promising it that you will be back… promising that very soon you will return to see what other gifts this inner sanctuary holds for you….

Now… making the journey out of your inner sanctuary… and back to this time and place… Taking your time… Feeling your feet solidly on the floor beneath you… Noticing how your chair feels against your legs… Breathing in and out at your own pace as you return to the sound of my voice… as you return to this moment in time….
And when you feel yourself fully present here again… open your eyes…
Take your time… I will wait for you… remembering that all is well…

Inner Guidance System (Your IGS)

I invite you to find a way to make your body comfortable… shifting your position if you need to… keeping your spine straight and supported as best you can… And as you shift into a more comfortable way of being, you may choose to close your eyes… or just keep a soft gaze downwards…

Take a deep breath… and as you exhale slowly… invite your body to relax… Take another deep breath… relaxing a little bit more with this exhale… making any sounds you need to make… One more deep breath… and relax… Ahhhhh… Scanning your body briefly and noticing if any place in your body feels tight or tense… Gently breathing into any part of your body that is holding tension or pain… Simply inviting it to release… and relax… just a little bit… and then just a little bit more…

Now take another breath… and as you exhale… give yourself permission to relax your mind… Let any thoughts or ideas just float away… As a new thought comes up in your mind… watch yourself let go of it… There's no need to hold on to any thoughts right now… Just let them go and continue to bring your attention back to your breathing… back to your relaxing… back to your breathing… back to your relaxing…

Taking another breath in… and as you exhale, imagine that you can move your awareness out of your mind… out of your head… and drop your awareness slowly down into your body… Letting it rest in the area of your solar plexus… your belly… for a moment…

And now… with the next breath… I invite you to let your awareness move into your very center… that's right… You are finding your center… finding your center… With every breath… as you exhale… you are beginning to allow yourself to move a little deeper… and a little deeper… until you come to rest in the deepest… most central place you can find within yourself… And now just allowing yourself to rest here for a moment…

This is the place where you have easy access to your own intuitive inner guidance system, your own IGS… It is always available to you here… If it feels good to you, go ahead and invite an image of your IGS to come forward in your imagination… It might appear as a person, real or imaginary… It might show up as an animal … or maybe it looks like something mechanical… a magical compass… or even a glossy high-tech device… Just allow whatever comes to you to be okay… and if nothing comes right now… know that's okay too…

Spending a little time with your own Inner Guidance System right now… whatever it looks or feels like to you…

You might decide to choose to ask your IGS what message it has for you right now in your life… What does your IGS want you to know?...

Being aware that if an answer comes… it might come visually… or in the form of a sound… or a color… or simply an awareness… an inner sense or knowing… Or it might come in words… Just allowing whatever bubbles forth to be okay… Or simply choosing to rest in the quietness…

Now finding a way to thank your IGS for its presence in your life… and for any specific help that it gave you today… Knowing that you can return here to the deepest center of your being where all knowing is available to you at any time… simply by closing your eyes… and taking a breath….

Bringing this deep sense of connection to your center… to your inner knowing,,, back here with you… Go ahead now and bring your awareness back up through your body… back to your breath… Feeling your breath now… Feeling your heart beating… Moving your awareness back up and up… back into your mind… back to your thinking mind…. back to your body…

Now finding some way to connect with your body again… Perhaps wiggling your toes or stretching your neck… Feeling your body fully supported by the chair… Now taking a deep breath and exhaling slowly…

Opening your eyes when you feel ready and coming back to our Circle… Take your time… I will wait for you… Remembering that all is well…

Walking Your Internal Red Carpet

Please take some time to settle into your body by focusing on your breath… Bring yourself home to yourself by breathing in and out… in your own rhythm… whatever that is for you today…

Letting your eyes softly close whenever you are ready… And in your imagination, I invite you to bring yourself to a very special place… indoors or outdoors… This is your own safe inner sanctuary where you can come to explore your inner world at any time…

Now that you are in your inner sanctuary, take a moment to lay down your own red carpet, just like they do for the big award shows and film openings… Making sure the carpet is very long and velvety and soft… You might add decorations like jewels or feathers or shimmering embroidery… I invite you to make this internal red carpet your very own so that it pleases you very much…

Now, if you choose to, slip into your most beautiful outfit… whatever you feel like wearing right now that will make you feel like a million bucks… Maybe even adding accessories… and don't forget your hair…

Very good… Now it's time to walk your own internal red carpet… so go ahead and bring yourself to the beginning of the carpet… And as you do, you find yourself noticing that lined up on either side of the carpet… as far as you can see… are all of your most adoring fans… You are realizing that, even when you're having a bad day or week, you do have a crowd of admirers who love to cheer you on….

Visualizing all of them now… your inner paparazzi, so to speak…
All of your Community members who offer or who have ever offered you love and encouragement and support… All of your inner Committee parts who exist to help you on your journey… Seeing your many Council spirit guides… Noticing any Animal Companions who have joined you here today… Allowing all of your fans to be present for you… Allowing them to cheer you on…

Taking a few moments now to stride down your inner red carpet alone… basking in the joy and well wishes of all your supporters and devotees… You might be called over to sign a few autographs… Don't hesitate… Let the love and adoration of all of your fans, both inner and outer, wash over you with gladness… and take some time to fully absorb their words of encouragement, their love…

Waving… waving to all your fans… continuing to walk your internal red carpet right up to the theatre that showcases your own blessed life… Gracefully walking up the steps of the theatre… Then turning around and blowing final kisses to the adoring crowd that has shown up today just for you…

And as you are waving… you find yourself
thanking them all for being present in your life…

Now you are entering the theatre…
offering gratitude for your life journey
that has brought you here today…

And now finding your way back here…
Taking a few slow deep breaths to bring
your body and mind back together…

As you slowly come back from this inner journey now…
know that you are bringing the admiration and praise that you just experienced… back with you into your daily life… allowing your adoring fans to accompany you through the rest of your day today…

Opening your eyes slowly… gently… when you are ready…
I will wait for you… Remembering that all is well…

Opening to Blossom

If it feels right, invite your eyes to softly close and then bring yourself to stillness … whatever that means for you today… Give yourself permission to come home to yourself for this next little while… Give yourself permission to come home to Spirit… to the One that holds the many parts of your world…. Give yourself permission to relax… even to relax just a little bit more… Paying attention to your breath…
Not trying to change it… Just noticing as you breathe in… and noticing as you breathe out… Breathing in the stillness that is always inside of you… Breathing out any inner chaos… Breathing in a radical acceptance… acceptance that embraces and encompasses all parts of you… And breathing out any thoughts that might be getting in the way of that acceptance… Giving yourself permission to just breathe in… to just breathe out… and to simply relax… just a little bit… and just a little bit more…

Now I invite you to imagine yourself in a beautiful spring garden…
Looking around and noticing that the trees and bushes are in new leaf…
a shiny bright green color that is so luscious to look at… There are flowers in new bloom everywhere… and you are smelling the fragrance of a new spring season… Walking around the garden… Looking… Listening…

Now you are coming to a stop in front of dark green bush… You may be noticing that the buds on this particular bush have not popped open yet… Crouching down in front of this bush… Observing swollen buds all over this bush… And now just resting one of these buds against the palm of your hand… gently…
Not taking the bud off of the bush…
Just letting it rest in your palm and observing its fullness…
Wondering if it is almost ready to burst open…

And as you are feeling the newness of this bud against your hand… I invite you to begin paying attention to a place inside of you… a place that is similar to this bud… A place inside you that is just about ready to blossom… to burst open with a full expression of growth… What is this place?… Can you name it?…
And what needs to happen in order for it to fully bloom?…

If you choose to, spend some time holding this inner part of you in the
center of your soul… Tenderly… Observing it as it is closed… and imagining what it will be like when it is fully open…

Now I invite you to slowly bring your attention back to the green bush…
and to the physical bud that is in the palm of your hand… Taking a moment now to thank it for its presence and for its gift to you today… Slowly standing… maybe even bowing to the bush that has not yet bloomed… Bowing also, to the inner part of you that is also getting ready to blossom…

And now taking a moment… preparing to leave this beautiful spring garden…
Coming back to your breath… Reminding yourself that you are in a body…
And now feel all the parts of your body against your chair…
Following the sound of my voice back to this present moment…

If it feels good… go ahead and stretch your body in any way that
brings you back to this moment… maybe just moving your head slowly
from side to side… Bringing yourself back into your body…
opening your eyes when you are ready…
Taking your time… I will wait for you…
Remembering that all is well…

Breaking Into Flower

Begin by making yourself as comfortable as you can… Closing your eyes when you are ready… or choosing to keep your eyes open with a soft downward gaze…

Giving the weight of your body over to the support of your chair… Leaning back… Surrendering… Giving the weight of your thoughts and feelings over to the presence of the Divine… however you imagine the Divine to be for your life right now…

And as you are relaxing more and more…
listen to these words by author, Rebecca West:

Were it possible for us to wait for ourselves to come into the room…
not many of us would find our hearts breaking into flower…
as we heard the door handle turn…

Now… as you are breathing in and out… as your thoughts are coming to stillness… as you are becoming more and more relaxed… I invite you to imagine yourself standing in a crowded room at a party… There is music in the background… People are talking in pairs and groups all around you… You are hearing laughter… and a savory aroma is coming from the kitchen…
Someone is refilling your glass with your favorite beverage…

The door into this room is opening now… and someone new is walking into the party… You find yourself looking up curiously… Who is arriving?… The door is all the way on the other side of the room so you cannot see the person clearly until they are a few feet away… You are moving closer to see who it is… And guess what?… It's you!

Imagine that you are watching this scene on your DVD player or other device, and you can press the Pause button… If you choose to, go ahead and pause this scene now… Imagining that the person who just walked into this party is you as your best, most wonderful, authentic, true self… What does this person look like?… What is he or she wearing?… How is this person holding their body?…

Now… taking a moment to look at yourself… the one who was already at the party… How are you reacting to your True Self who just showed up?… Are you about to turn away?… Are you thinking about finding someone more interesting to talk with?…

or… as Rebecca West so poignantly writes…
is your heart breaking into flower
at this very connection with yourself?…

Take some time now to simply be with this true, authentic you…
And see if you can allow your heart to break into flower at this precious inner connection… even just a little bit… and maybe just a little bit more…

Now it is time to start thinking about leaving the party…
So find a way to thank your beautiful authentic self…
bowing to yourself if you like…
feeling so full of self-acceptance and gladness
to be exactly who you are…

And then bringing yourself back slowly… slowly…
back to the present moment…
Following the sound of my voice…
Becoming aware of your own steady breath…
Noticing that you are in a physical body…
Maybe wiggling your fingers and toes…
or giving yourself a big stretch…

When you are ready…
go ahead and open your eyes…
Take your time…
I will wait for you…
Remembering that all is well…

The Puzzle of Your Life – Part 1

Begin by making yourself as comfortable as you can right now…
Please listen to your body and respect whatever it is asking you for
in this moment…

I invite you to gently close your eyes whenever you feel ready to do so…
Or keep a soft steady gaze, looking down… And now try focusing on your breath for a moment… Feel the air flowing in and out of your nostrils… in… and out… in… and out… Feel your chest rising and falling with each breath…
rising and falling… rising and falling…

Now you are feeling a bit more relaxed… And in your imagination I invite you to take yourself to your own inner sanctuary… a safe place… created by and for you… It might be a place you already know… or it might be a purely imaginary place… Taking yourself there now… Walking around… Noticing what you see… what you can hear… what you can smell… what you can feel… Remembering that this is a completely safe place…

If it feels right, go ahead and invite one of your Guides to join you… This might be a religious figure… or a goddess of some sort… It might be a fictional character whose wisdom resonates with you… It might be someone in your life whose wisdom has touched you… It might even be a being from one of your SoulCollage® cards… Just saying hello to your Guide now, thanking him or her for coming…
Knowing that you are completely safe at all times with him or her…

Now your guide is leading you to your inner workroom… This is a place inside your inner sanctuary where you can take a look at what's going on in your life… Walking there… to the Workroom… with your Guide now… and when you arrive… noticing that there is a jigsaw puzzle spread out and incomplete on a large work table in the center of your workroom… Your Guide tells you that this puzzle represents your own life…

As you are examining the puzzle of your life with your Guide… you might be noticing that some of the pieces you put in a while ago still fit… but they are the wrong color for the design… Or maybe you are noticing that a piece that used to fit no longer fits when the correct piece on the other side is added in…

As you become aware of these pieces that don't fit… take a moment to ask your guide to help you remove or reconfigure them… maybe not right now… but as you go through your life… Your Guide's assistance will be appreciated… and you are realizing also that you never have to do this inner work alone…

You might be noticing now that the border of your jigsaw puzzle is actually complete… That's right… You are seeing that all the pieces that make up the edges of your puzzle are connected… creating a perfect border… You seem surprised about this… and your Guide tells you that the border of your puzzle represents love… You are becoming aware that the boundary of your own life journey… is also bordered with love… Allowing time to absorb this realization…
that the boundary of your own life journey is bordered with love…
It always has been… It is now… It always will be…

Taking a moment now to allow your Guide to point out anything else
you need to know… about this beautiful jigsaw puzzle that depicts your life…

You might want to ask a question about one or two of the specific pieces that make up your life… and listen for whatever wisdom your Guide wants to share with you…

It is time to start thinking about leaving your inner workroom now, so if you like… take a moment to thank your Guide for joining you… Knowing that you can return here whenever you want… simply by closing your eyes and taking a breath…

And when you are ready… slowly… slowly… bring yourself back to the sound of my voice… bringing your attention back into your body… maybe stretching a little bit… or yawning… doing whatever you need to in order to be fully present once again with us…

Gently opening your eyes when you are comfortable doing so…
Taking your time… I will wait for you…
Remembering that all is well…

The Puzzle of Your Life - Part 2

Please begin by taking a few moments to consciously relax your body… Coming in to the present moment… Letting go of what you've been doing… and letting go of whatever comes next… Just using your breath to sink into this moment right here… right now… Adjusting any part of your body to make yourself even more comfortable… Giving yourself permission to relax your body and also to relax your mind… Giving yourself permission to look inward for this next little while…

And now in your imagination… I invite you to go back to your inner sanctuary… finding your Guide… Maybe it's the same Guide that you met in the first meditation… or maybe you are joined by a different Guide… Let it be what it is… And just take a moment now to go for a walk outside your sanctuary… with your Guide… You might choose to walk in silence… absorbing his or her strength and comfort as you go… or you might have a question you want to ask about your own life…
or about a piece of your life…

Now, if you choose to, go ahead and bring yourself and your Guide back to your inner workroom… You are seeing your jigsaw puzzle spread out over the table… bordered with love… all the edges complete… the inside continuing to take shape…

This time you are surprised to notice that a few of your cherished personal Community members are here in the workroom with you… You might be seeing some close family members… or friends… You might even be seeing a few people who have passed on… simply paying attention to how good it feels that they can join you here today…

And as you look around… you are realizing that they are working on your puzzle too… If you choose to… go ahead and join them… Experience sifting through the various pieces of your life together with them… and together… finding ways to make some more of the pieces fit…

Now you are noticing that your jigsaw puzzle also includes some of the puzzle pieces of these others who are close to you in your real life… Listening to your Guide as he or she says… "Love is to be the border around our lives… Love is to be the boundary of our being"… Taking a moment now to fully absorb the fact that love is also the border around our collective, communal lives…

If it feels good… link arms or hold hands with the Community members who have joined you here today… forming a circle around the worktable where the puzzle of your life rests… Holding hands… Your Guide is next to you… and everyone else who cares about your life is here as well… You are all gazing at your puzzle together…

Standing here… an integral part of this circle… you are noticing that your puzzle is not completely put together yet… There are pieces missing… and there are still some pieces that used to fit but now do not… Yet you are realizing that this doesn't mar the beauty of the whole picture of the puzzle that is your life… You are becoming aware that you can and do accept this puzzle… your puzzle… exactly as it is… because you are the one who is creating it… and these others … and your Guide… are helping you… You are filled with the knowing that you don't ever need to work on this puzzle of your life alone…

I invite you now to find a way to thank these Community members for joining you today… and for the pieces they have added to your puzzle… Also thanking your Guide… Knowing that you can return to this sanctuary… to this workroom and this puzzle… any time you like simply by closing your eyes and taking a breath…

And when you are ready… slowly… slowly… bring yourself back to the sound of my voice… bringing your attention back into your body… maybe stretching a little bit… or yawning… just doing whatever you need to in order to be fully present once again with us…

Gently opening your eyes when you are comfortable doing so…
Taking your time… I will wait for you… Remembering that all is well…

Part 2

Be Here Now

*It is the imagination
that lights the slow fuse of the possible.*

~ Emily Dickinson

Be Here Now

Please sit comfortably in your chair with your feet flat on the floor to ground you… Sitting up straight and tall… Surrendering your body into the safety of the furniture that is supporting you…

Taking a deep breath in… and letting it go… Taking another deep breath in… exhaling completely… Taking another breath in… and letting it go… Ahhh… Continuing to breathe in and out… at your own pace now… If it feels comfortable… go ahead and gently close your eyes… shutting out all the distractions of your daily life… just for a little while…

Letting your body relax just a little bit more with each breath… Inhaling relaxation… and exhaling any tension that might be making its home in your body or mind… Inhaling relaxation… and exhaling tension… Allowing yourself to be more and more calm and relaxed…. with each breath…

I invite you to remember that the imagination is a powerful tool… and you can access yours at any time… in any circumstance… So with this in mind… use your imagination to take yourself to your favorite place in nature… a place where you feel most at home with yourself…

Taking yourself to this beautiful, peaceful place and just walking around a bit… absorbing the sights… the sounds… any fragrances in the air… Maybe stooping to pick a flower or hold a shell or special stone…

And now… as you are walking around this special place… you find yourself standing in front of a lovely bench… Pausing for a moment when you find it… Noticing what color it is… what it's made of… how big it is… And now, noticing that you need a little rest… go ahead and sit yourself down right in the middle of the bench… which is there to hold you… to support you… on this journey…

You are sitting in the center of this bench… simply focusing on your breath… as it flows in… and out… resting in your breath… and in the peace… Noticing any thoughts that are floating to the surface of your mind… just noticing them… accepting them… just watching them come and go… thanking each thought for coming and then watching it leave… and in between the thoughts… just resting in the silence…

Now you are noticing that two beings have come to join you on your bench… One is sitting on your left… and the other is on your right… They feel friendly and safe to you… I invite you now to turn towards the figure on your left… This is the Past You… This is the you that you were yesterday… or last year… Take a look at this part of you now… and listen… What is he or she saying to you?... The Past You might be talking about regrets… or happy memories… or transformation… Just listening now… not judging this part of you or trying to talk back to it… It is a valid part of you, this Past You… It has important information to give you… Just listening… accepting… feeling whatever you are feeling… and letting it all be okay…

And now… having listened to this part of you from the past… nod or bow to it… and then if it feels okay to you… turn to the figure on your right… This is the Future You… This is the you that you will be tomorrow… or the next day…or a year from now… Taking a look at this part of you… Listening in… What is your Future Self saying to you right now?... Future You might be telling you all the things you have to do to get to where he or she is in the future… This part of you might be telling you all the things that could possibly happen between now and then… Just listening for now… Not judging this part of you or trying to talk back to it… This Future Self is a valid part of you… It has important information to give you… Just listening now… accepting… feeling whatever you are feeling… and letting it all be okay…

Now… still sitting in the middle of your bench…with the Past You on your left and the Future You on your right… Firmly tell these two parts of you that you'd like a little more space… and ask them to move farther away from you on the bench… In your imagination, you can make the bench longer or wider if you need to… Just noticing how it feels to have a good amount of space between your past… and the now… and your future…

If it feels good… go ahead and thank this Past Self and this Future Self for joining you today… And then ask them to take a walk and leave you alone for a while… Notice how easily they get up and walk away after they've been listened to thoroughly…

And now notice how it feels to be free of the Past You and the Future You for a while… Just sitting on the bench… Just your own beautiful self in the here and now… The past is gone and the future is absent… You are sitting in this beautiful space and inhabiting this beautiful moment right here and now…

And you can feel how precious this present moment is...
You are simply being... You are simply being here...
You are simply being here now...

Savoring the quiet in and out flow of your breath...
resting in the present moment... feeling fully present and fully alive...

If the Past You or Future You venture back to whisper in your ear...
just notice this and acknowledge them... and then let them go...
Resting in the inhale... Resting in the exhale...
Resting in this moment... the only moment that matters...

And now, rising from your bench... Taking in the beautiful view you've created here...
Knowing you can come back at any time... just by closing your eyes and imagining it...

Finding a gentle way now to bring yourself back into your physical body...
Feeling your feet on the floor, noticing the position your legs are in, feeling y
our back against the chair... Maybe slowly moving your head from side to side...
shaking out your hands... or wiggling your feet and legs...
Following the sound of my voice back to this room, this place, this time...

And when you are ready... gently opening your eyes...
There is no rush... I will wait for you... Take your time...
Remembering that all is well...

Velvet Blanket

When you are ready, allow yourself to come to stillness… Give yourself permission to come home to yourself for these next few minutes… I invite you to give yourself permission to come home to Spirit… to the One that holds the many parts of your world… Giving yourself permission to relax for now… paying attention to your breath… not trying to change it… just paying attention… just noticing the air flowing in as you inhale… and noticing the air flowing out as you exhale… Breathing in the stillness that is always inside of you… breathing out any inner chaos… Breathing in peace… and breathing out any inner conflicts that have been going on lately for you… Simply breathing in… and out… in… and out…

Now imagine that lying before you is a large blanket made of soft plush velvet… This blanket is always, always here for you… in your imagination… Looking at the blanket right now… and noticing what color it is today…

If you like, go ahead and run your hands over this soft, luxurious blanket… feeling its texture… lifting it to your nose if you want to and inhaling its scent… What does it smell like to you?… Breathing it in… Savoring the scent… and texture… and color… of this velvet blanket…

And then… if you choose to… pick the blanket up gently in your hands and wrap it around your whole body… You are seeing that it is large enough to cover you with more left over… Once you are enveloped in your own personal velvet blanket… maybe you'd like to lie down or sit down with it still wrapped around you… or you can continue to stay standing if you prefer…

Spending these next few minutes with your velvet blanket… Allowing its warmth and silky comfort to envelop your whole body… envelop your whole mind… your whole spirit… Noticing any parts of your body that are tight… and allowing them to relax… to completely relax under the beauty of this comfortable blanket that is soothing your body…. your mind… and your spirit…

Taking this time just for you… enveloped in your velvet blanket… allowing its softness to help you soften on the inside too… just a little bit somewhere…

And you are noticing that the velvet blanket is softening your heart a little bit… in just the right places that need to be softened today… The softness of this blanket is softening and relaxing your mind… It is calming your thoughts as well…

The blanket is gentling your body… It is giving you permission to relax even just a little bit more… It is giving you permission to continue to envelop yourself in comfort and beauty… which you so deserve…

It's almost time to start thinking about coming back from this inner journey… so go ahead and take a moment to thank your blanket for being there for you… and if you like… name the gift that you received from your blanket today… maybe it was peace… perhaps comfort… or simply a much needed rest… Naming the gift that you received today…

And as you are preparing to return… you can either choose to keep the blanket wrapped around you… or you can take the blanket off… knowing that it will always be here for you in your imagination… It will always be exactly the right color that you need in that moment…

I invite you now to come back to your breath… Notice the air as it comes into your body and fills your lungs… Then notice how it feels to release the breath through your nose or mouth… maybe releasing the breath with a sound or a sigh… remembering where you are… noticing the feel of your feet… legs… hip… back… neck… head…

And following the sound of my voice back to this present moment… If it feels good to do so, you might want to stretch your legs and arms… maybe move your head slowly from side to side… grounding yourself back into your body in whatever way feels just right to you in this moment…

When you feel ready… you can gently open your eyes…
taking your time… I will wait for you…
Remembering that all is well.

Lotus Flower of Self-Blessing

Begin by getting as comfortable as you can…
and closing your eyes when you are ready…
or you might prefer to keep a soft gaze downwards…
whatever feels right to you today…

Giving the weight of your body
over to the support of the chair you are in…
resting… surrendering… and also…
giving the weight of your thoughts and feelings
over to the presence of the Divine…
however you imagine the Divine to be for your life right now…

As you breathe in and out … as your thoughts are coming to stillness…
as you become more and more relaxed… I invite you to imagine yourself near
a beautiful pond… Notice the weather… Can you tell if it is daytime or nighttime?…
Find a place to sit on the edge of this pond… What sounds do you hear?...
What do you see?… Are there any animals or insects present with you…
as you sit quietly by this lovely little pond?...

Taking a closer look at the surface of the water… you are noticing one beautiful
lotus flower close to you… It seems to be beckoning to you… What color is this
lotus?… As you are paying attention to its color… you are also noticing the layering
of so many petals opening out from its center… noticing that this lotus has grown
up through the mud at the bottom of this pond… and has turned into a gorgeous
flower… just for you…

Now… in your imagination where all things are possible… you are noticing that
you are becoming smaller in size… and then a bit smaller… until you are just the
right size to hop over to this lotus… your lotus… and sit in the center of it… Ahhhh…
Noticing how at home you feel here… Taking a moment to observe the petals that
now surround you… Each of these petals represents a part of yourself… a part of
your soul… Some of the petals may be whole and lush… Some of them may be a bit
withered or damaged by the sun or by bugs or whatever… but each of the petals is
yours… Each of these petals has something precious to give to the life of your soul…
Each petal contributes to the whole of you… to the whole of your flower…

I invite you to listen to these words from the poet Galway Kinnell now:

> *The bud*
> *stands for all things,*
> *for everything flowers, from within, of self-blessing;*
> *though sometimes it is necessary*
> *to reteach a thing its loveliness,*
> *to put a hand on the brow*
> *of the flower*
> *and retell it in words and in touch*
> *it is lovely*
> *until it flowers again from within, of self-blessing…*

Knowing within that where you are sitting right now… is your place of self-blessing… So just resting here for a while… in the center of your lotus blossom… and listening to the whispering petals of your soul… knowing that they are blessing you… You are listening to them… You are feeling their love… and… if you choose… you are inviting their wisdom…

This is the place where you can… whenever you choose to… return again and again to reteach yourself your loveliness… This is the place where you can rest in the sanctuary and safety of your own soul…

Now it is nearing time to leave this pond… and your lotus flower… So find a way to thank your flower… Maybe even bowing to the petals one by one… or blowing them kisses… feeling so full of gratitude and grace… feeling so full of self-acceptance and gladness to be exactly who you are…

And now you are sensing your body getting a little bit bigger… and bigger… until you are your normal size now… leaving the pond behind… and coming back to the present moment… following the sound of my voice… hearing your own steady breath… noticing how your legs and back feel resting against the chair… becoming more and more aware of your surroundings… Maybe wiggling your fingers and toes… Maybe stretching your arms and your legs… Rolling your neck from side to side if that feels good to you…

And when you are ready… only when you are ready… opening your eyes… taking your time… I will wait for you… There is no rush… Remembering that all is well…

Touching Peace

If it feels good, take a deep breath… in… and out… And just give your body permission to relax and be comfortable for this next little while…

Allow your body to experience the contact that it makes with the chair and with the floor… and let it adjust itself in any way it needs to in order to be just a little bit more comfortable… Shifting any part of you that needs to move for that settled feeling of ahhh… You can close your eyes when it feels safe and comfortable to do so… or you might choose to keep a soft gaze downwards…

As you tune in to the rhythm of your breathing, imagine that when you inhale… you're inhaling a little bit of the sky… and it's very clear and very refreshing… And as you exhale, imagine that you're letting go of whatever you don't need right now… Inhaling the light, clear sky… Exhaling that which does not serve you right now…

Letting the rhythm of your breath be just what it is… a simple and beautiful process of taking in what's fresh and clear… and letting go of what's no longer needed…

Each breath you take relaxes and refreshes you… Your breathing and your mind are becoming clearer and clearer… Your body is relaxing a little bit more with each inhale and exhale…

Allowing your imagination to be open and receptive… Continuing to breathe in… and breathe out… I invite you to take a little journey now… a magical journey to your inner world where you are always safe… where everything is always exactly as it should be…

And in your imagination… if you choose… take yourself to a large beautiful lake…

You find yourself walking around the shore of the lake… The sky is clear… Noticing if it is daytime or night time… Is the sun shining… or is the moon luminescent on the water?… What are you noticing here besides the water?… What sounds do you hear?… What scents are sweet to inhale?… Noticing how your body feels near this lake… Maybe it is looser… Maybe it's more relaxed… Or maybe it's feeling something else… Let it all be okay…

Take a moment to pause and look at the water that makes up this inner lake… Now… using your imagination… if you choose to… go ahead and step into the water… or stay on the shore if you choose that… Give yourself permission to step into the shallow water… or to stand on the edge of it…

If you are choosing to enter the lake… know that it doesn't matter what you are wearing… because this is an inner journey… so just stepping into the water and now continuing to walk out to the center of the lake… If you want to swim to the center of the lake, that's okay too… This is all happening in your own imagination so you can control whatever happens here… The waters are safe… You are safe… And if you are standing on shore… perhaps you can just watch yourself walking to the center of the lake… or you can choose to meander around the edge of the lake for the next little while… and see what there is to see…

Now… if you are in the lake… when you find yourself in the middle of the lake… go ahead and dive down… down… all the way down to the bottom of your warm, calm lake… As you slip through the water… you are surrounded by a profound silence… and you are awed to see that the bottom of the lake bed is carpeted with beautiful white pearls… If you want to, go ahead and lightly touch one of those pearls now… simply touch it… knowing that as you are touching it… you are touching a deep peace that always… always lives inside of you…

Now picking up just one of these shimmering pearls and holding it in your hand… As you do so, the knowledge comes to you that at any time your world becomes chaotic or out of control… you can dive down deep right here in this inner lake and touch peace… because peace lives right here… inside of you… all the time… just waiting for you to sense and feel and touch it…

If you want to hold onto this pearl that you have picked up, you can do so… knowing that there are many more for you to find when you return… And now you are swimming back up to the surface of the lake… and swimming or walking back to the shore… Bringing yourself back to dry land now…

Drying yourself off by the water's edge… and now spending a few more moments in silence near your beautiful inner lake… Remembering that all you need to do to touch peace is to dive… or float down… into its center…

Now it's time to start thinking about leaving your inner lake… so… I invite you to focus a little more closely on the sound of my voice… following the sound of my voice back to this present moment… paying attention once again to your breath… remembering that you are not just in your imagination but that you are in a body as well… breathing a little more deeply and consciously…

You might want to shift in your chair… Stretch your body in any way that feels good to you…

Opening your eyes when you are ready to do so… Taking your time… I will wait for you… Remembering that all is well.

The Mirror

Taking a deep breath and allowing your eyes to close… Giving your body permission to relax and be comfortable… As comfortable as it can be right now…

Allowing your body to feel… really feel… the contact that it makes with the chair and with the floor… and letting your body adjust itself in any way it needs to… in order to be even a bit more comfortable for now…

As you tune in to the rhythm of your breathing, imagine that when you inhale… you're inhaling a little bit of the sky… and it's very clear and very refreshing… And as you exhale, imagine that you're letting go of whatever you don't need right now… Inhaling the light, clear sky…
Exhaling that which does not serve you right now…

Letting the rhythm of your breath be just what it is… a simple and beautiful process of taking in what's fresh and clear… and letting go of what's no longer needed…

Each breath you take relaxes and refreshes you… Your breathing and your mind are becoming clearer and clearer… Your body is relaxing a little bit more with each inhale and exhale…

Now… in your mind's eye… I invite you to imagine a large mirror… It can be any shape… and made of any materials that you want it to be made of… as long as it's a large full-length mirror… You can see it standing several feet away from you now… and you are imagining yourself standing up and walking slowly… very slowly… over to this beautiful mirror…

Noticing how you are feeling as you are walking towards the mirror… just noticing… and accepting however you are feeling about looking at yourself in this mirror… Accepting your feelings… your thoughts… Not judging whatever is going on inside you… Treating it all with kindness… It's all okay… You are truly safe here…

And now you are standing in front of the mirror… gazing at your reflection for a moment… and as you're looking… I invite you to listen to these words from Saraha… one of the greatest yogis of India in the late 8th century:

Here in this body are the sacred rivers…
here are the sun and moon as well as all the pilgrimage places…

I have not encountered another temple as blissful as my own body…

Noticing now how it feels to think of your own body as a temple… a sacred place…

We're going to scan the sacred rivers of our bodies now… We're going to offer our often-neglected bodies some attention… some kindness and love… some gratitude…

Starting with your feet… See them in the mirror, really see your feet… Thank your feet for all the places they have taken you… all the journeys they have led you through…

Sacred rivers, pilgrimage places… sacred rivers, pilgrimage places…

Now look at your legs… Really see your legs… How have they held you up lately?… How have they supported you?… And thank your legs for their service to you…

Spending some time now looking at your hips and pelvic area… See your hips, really look at your pelvis for a moment… What pleasures have these parts of your body given you throughout your life?… Have they helped you bear children?… Have they given you sexual pleasure?… Take some time to thank your hips and your pelvis… for all that they have done for you over the years…

Sacred rivers, pilgrimage places… sacred rivers, pilgrimage places…

Now it's time to look at your stomach… See your stomach, really see it… Maybe place your hands on it if that feels good to you… Just spend a moment appreciating your stomach… How has your stomach served you throughout your life?… Can you find it in your heart to thank it for its service to you?…

Spending a little time now gazing at your chest… Really looking at your chest in the mirror… Leaving behind any judgments coming from any of your Inner Committee members… Leaving behind any criticisms for now… How has your chest served you?… If you are a woman, have your breasts given you pleasure?… Have they been a source of nourishment for a baby?… Also noting that your chest contains your heart… and your lungs… taking some time now to shower your chest…
your heart… your lungs… with appreciation and gratitude…

Sacred rivers, pilgrimage places… sacred rivers, pilgrimage places…

Now your arms… look at them in your imaginary mirror… and your hands…
How have your arms and hands assisted you in your life lately?…
Holding… reaching… healing… soothing…

And now gladly thanking your arms and hands for their service to you…

And finally… your head… Gaze for a moment into your own eyes…
What color are they?… Thank your eyes for their gift of sight… And your mouth…
Is it smiling?… Thanking your lips and tongue… your nose… throat and larynx…
Thank them all for working together to serve you through your five senses…

Sacred rivers, pilgrimage places… sacred rivers, pilgrimage places…

Now looking at your whole body for a moment again in the mirror…
Your beautiful body… made up of skin and bones… muscle and tissue…
cells and memory… Sacred rivers… Pilgrimage places… Your whole body…..

Placing your hands together in prayer position, in front of your chest…
bowing to yourself… your magnificent, beautiful self… and spending a moment
thanking your body… for being a blissful temple for your spirit… all these years…
It's time to come back to this time and place now… Finding a way to thank your mirror
for its true reflections today… paying attention to your breath once again… feeling
your chest rising and falling with each breath… noticing how your body feels against
the chair you're sitting in… feeling your feet against the floor…
maybe even stretching gently a little bit in your own way…

And now… gently opening your eyes whenever you are ready…
taking your time… I will wait for you…
Remembering that all is well…

Light Up Your Holidays

I invite you to rest for a few moments now… Taking a deep breath in… and letting it out with sigh or some other sound… letting your breathing be whatever it wants to be today… holding the intention of being kind to yourself for the next few minutes… adjusting your body however it needs so that you can become just a little bit more comfortable… just a little bit more relaxed… continuing to breathe in… and breathe out… in… and out… in… and out…

Now, if you like… imagine yourself walking through a quiet forest… It is nighttime and it is dark… but you can see some starlight and moon glow high above you… through the trees… It feels peaceful here… and very safe… As you are walking slowly through the woods… you are leaving behind all of the stress and buzz of the holidays… the crowded malls… the long lines at the post office… and all of the to-do lists… You are leaving all of that behind you now as you walk through this beautiful forest… Looking around carefully… What are you noticing?… Is there snow on the ground… or not…? Are there animals hiding in the trees?… What are you seeing?… What sounds are making themselves known to you?… What are you smelling in the air?… What are you feeling?..

Now you are approaching a large well-lit clearing… It is still several steps away… And as you walk into this clearing… you are noticing that there is someone in the center of it... This is a very wise being… and it is someone who has come here today specifically to meet you… Moving a little closer… Finding out who it is in the center of the clearing… It might be an angel… It might even be Saint Nicholas… or someone from your past... a very special spirit guide… or an animal totem… Who is here for you today in the center of this inner clearing?…

You are hearing this wise being calling your name now… And if you choose to… go to him or her… and spend a few moments listening… This wise one has some important things to tell you about light and your soul and the holidays… so just listen while they talk with you… They might have some specific insights to give you about your own particular upcoming holidays… whatever that means for you…

Asking this being a question… if that feels right to you… or simply listening…

It's almost time to leave now… so find a way to say good-bye to this wise being… and know that you are not leaving for good… Know that you can come back to this magical place any time you want or need to… This wise being is your special companion… and will guide you and comfort you… any time you ask…

Saying good-bye to each other for now… and then looking for the path you came in on… You will be able to find the path because your special wise companion has left a lantern… and a beautifully wrapped gift for you there…
Taking a moment now to unwrap the gift… See what this wise one has chosen to give you as a special gift… And now picking up the lantern… and returning home through the woods with your gift… taking your time coming back…

When you are back… take a few deep breaths… Feel your legs and your back against the chair… Notice your feet on the floor… Coming back to your body in any way that feels good to you… Open your eyes when you are ready… Taking your time…
I will wait for you… Remembering that all is well…

Lucky Leprechaun

When you are ready, allow yourself to come to stillness… Try giving yourself permission to come home to yourself for these next few minutes… Giving yourself permission to simply relax a little bit… Paying attention to your breath… Not trying to change it… Just noticing as you breathe in… and noticing as you breathe out… Breathing in peace… Breathing out any inner chaos… Breathing in peace… Breathing out any inner conflict… Giving yourself permission to do nothing right now except inhale… and exhale… inhale… and exhale…

In your imagination… bring yourself to a beautiful outdoor space… imagining that it is a bright and sunny day… looking around… exploring a little bit… this safe place you've created for yourself in nature…

Slowly you are noticing in the sky… a wide and colorful rainbow… You might be feeling delighted and excited like a child… to see this rainbow so close to you… If you'd like to… go ahead and start walking closer to it… and closer… and closer…

You are now standing at the edge of this bright, amazing rainbow… Allowing its colors to shimmer and shine around you and within you… How are you feeling, sheltered by this rainbow?… Just noticing any places in your body that feel open and receptive to the colors of your rainbow…

And now… walking alongside your rainbow… all the way to the other end of it… And here… at the end of the rainbow… you are seeing… just like the legends say… a big pot of gold… And this big pot of gold is just for you… What are you thinking about this pot of gold?… Noticing your thoughts… just noticing…

And now slowly… like magic… a little leprechaun dressed in green appears beside your pot of gold… You see that there is a lucky four-leaf clover sprouting up from his sparkly hat…

If it feels right, go ahead and introduce yourself to this leprechaun… And now hear him say that he is delighted to meet you… He says that his name is Lucky Leprechaun… and he is here to help you remember all the ways that you are lucky… all the ways that good fortune is part of your life… all the ways that you are blessed… He is telling you that sometimes we get so busy in our lives… and with our to-do lists… that we forget what's in our own personal pot of gold…

Watching now as Lucky Leprechaun pulls out each shiny coin from your own personal

pot of gold… one by one… and listening as he names your lucky blessings one by one… You're lucky because… You've been blessed with… It's your good fortune to…

After a while… Lucky Leprechaun invites you to go ahead and pick some of those golden coins out of the pot yourself… So if you want to… do that now… naming each one with gladness… I'm lucky because… I've been blessed with… It's my good fortune to… And with each coin you are naming a lucky blessing…

It's time to start thinking about leaving the pot of gold now… so find a way to thank your Lucky Leprechaun for being here for you today… and for reminding you how lucky you really are… knowing that you can come back to this rainbow and this pot of gold at any time… to immerse yourself in gratitude… and to remind yourself how lucky you really are… simply by taking a breath… and opening your imagination…

And now taking a moment… coming back to your breath… sensing all the parts of your body against your chair… following the sound of my voice back to this present moment… If it feels good to do so, try stretching any part of your body that needs gentle movement… bringing yourself back into your body… grounding yourself back in current time… and opening your eyes when you feel ready… Take your time… I will wait for you… All is well…

Table of Creativity

Please take a moment now to put down anything you're holding in your hands… Shake out your hands lightly and then hold them to your heart for a moment… Taking a deep breath in and out… Closing your eyes… Maybe even saying hello to yourself… Enjoying this feeling of centering… Maybe even smiling to yourself as you give yourself permission to spend this next little while opening your imagination… opening to your own creative self…

And just as you've put down what was in your hands… go ahead and try putting down anything that you are carrying in your mind… setting down any thoughts that are getting in the way of being present right now… Just putting it all down for now… and noticing how much lighter your mind and spirit are for this…

Paying attention to your breath… not trying to change it… just being present with yourself… giving yourself permission now to be open to the magic of possibility…

In your imagination, I invite you to see yourself standing in a large room… any room you'd like… Make it as big as you can… You are standing just inside the door… and way over there… on the other side of the room… you can see a very large table… The Table of Creativity is over there by the windows on the other side of the room… and this Table is much, much bigger than the biggest dining table you can imagine…

You are sensing light… and color… and your favorite music over there… on the other side of the room by the Table… You are starting to make your way over to the Table of Creativity… but you find that you are being blocked by three people or beings… They might be clearly visible to you… or they might be shadowy and unknown… And you are stopping now in front of these three beings for a moment…

The being on the left is your Inner Critic… Take notice of him or her now… What is this part of you saying to you about your creativity?…

The being in the middle is your Inner Perfectionist… Take notice of him or her now… What is this part of you saying to you about your creativity?…

And finally… the being on the right is your Inner Serious One… Take notice of him or her now… What is this part of you saying to you about your creativity?…

Even if you can't see their faces… even if you don't know their names… their energy is still recognizable to you… I invite you now to take a minute or so to stand with these three… And if you choose to do this… look each one in the eye and say… "I hear you. Thank you for your input"… If that doesn't feel good to you right now, that's okay too… You don't have to speak to them if you don't want to…

Now I invite you to say to them… "I hear you… and I am choosing to move to the Table of Creativity now… I have decided to take this time to discover what is on that Table for me"… And after saying this… you notice that they are either fading quietly away… or they are obeying your request to go outside for a cup of tea or a nice long walk…

As they are leaving… you are noticing that the room is becoming much brighter… and you feel much freer… now that these inner parts are no longer blocking you from the Table of Creativity… You are sensing that this huge table on the other side of the room is beckoning to you… so skip on over there now… or run or walk or dance… whatever movement feels good to you in this moment…

Arriving at the large table… you observe that it is covered with all kinds of wonderful things that might enhance your creativity… Taking a slow walk all around the table… seeing everything that is there… Here are some things that might be there for you… Listen and look as I read them… knowing that creativity takes many, many forms…

Perhaps you are seeing paints… crayons… chalk… notepads… pens… colored pencils… clay… a computer… glitter… musical instruments… a microphone… mixing bowls… swatches of fabric… scissors… beautiful images torn from magazines… card stock… handmade paper… carpentry tools… a sewing machine… books… ribbon… construction paper… yarn… needles and thread… knitting needles… musical instruments… a camera… crochet hooks… measuring spoons… a rolling pin… What else is there on this table that is calling to your creative soul?…

Now… when you are ready… and if it feels right… go ahead and take something off of the table… just one thing… You may be discovering that many things are calling to you… but for now… just take one thing off of the Table… and cradle it in your hands like the gift that it is… spending a moment with it… maybe sensing memories of a time when you used this creative tool in the past… maybe sensing into how you can use this tool in your current life situation… If other things on the table are also calling to you… know that you can come back to this table and its gifts at any time…

Whatever you've taken from the table… go ahead and ask it what it would like you to do with it next… waiting for the answer… Remembering that your Inner Critic…

Perfectionist… and Serious One… are not blocking you anymore…
You are here… right now… nurturing your own inner creative flame…

Listening… just listening… What does this item want you to do with it?…
What does it need from you?… How can it serve you?…

And maybe setting an intention in your heart… What is your next creative step going to be?… Let it be a tiny baby step… nothing too big… just one little thing you'll easily be able to do in the coming week… with this item…
to help wake up your own creative self…

Now it's time to begin to think about leaving this inner space… so if you like… bow to your Table of Creativity… thank it for its presence in your imagination… knowing that you can return here any time you like just by closing your eyes and taking a breath…

Carrying the item you took from the table with you… walking or dancing back across the large room… and out the door where you entered…
bringing yourself back into this day and time…
following the sound of my voice…

Coming back to your body and your breath…
maybe taking a moment to stretch your body in some way…
grounding yourself back in this moment… opening your eyes gently
when you feel ready… I will wait for you… Take your time…
Remembering that all is well…

Part 3

Inner Voices

Imagination will often carry us to worlds that never were. But without it, we go nowhere.

~ Carl Sagan

Magic Bus Ride

Begin by making yourself as comfortable as you can… Taking a few deep breaths… just noticing your body and how it is feeling right now… acknowledging yourself for taking the time to come here today… Breathing in… and breathing out… Listening to the sound of your breath… Feeling the beating of your heart… Breathing in… and breathing out… There's nothing to do right now… There's nowhere to go but here… Noticing if there's any part of your body that is tight or uncomfortable… and just breathing for a moment into that part of your body… or adjusting your position until that part is able to relax just a little bit more… Breathing in… and out… You are becoming more and more relaxed… Breathing in… breathing out…

Now I invite you to imagine yourself walking in a place that you love… a city… or near the ocean… in the woods… or even your own back yard… You are walking… and taking in all the sounds and sights that are around you… Taking your time… just walking… just a little bit curious about what you'll discover on this walk…

Pretty soon you are coming upon a bus… This is the bus that is holding your Inner Committee members… They are all on this bus… It is parked… not moving… and you find yourself stopping when you are about 10-20 feet away from it… and now you are simply looking at your Inner Committee bus…

Noticing what color it is… School busses are yellow… and transit busses are usually blue and silver… but what color is your bus?…

Busses usually have writing on them… either on the sides, indicating where they came from… or on the front above the windshield… describing where they are going… Does your bus have any writing on it?…

Feel free to walk all the way around your bus now… looking at it from all sides… remembering that inside this bus are all of your Inner Committee members… And just taking a moment to notice how you are feeling about this bus… Are you curious?… Maybe a little anxious?… Treating any feelings that are coming up for you with kindness… and also remembering that this is a perfectly safe place… and that you are the one in charge of this inner journey… It is your journey… yours alone…

Now if you choose to… and only if you choose too… go ahead and approach the bus… pausing when you reach the door… knocking three times on the door and watching as it opens to you from the inside… climbing the three steps into the bus…

And taking a look at the driver's seat… Is one of your inner parts sitting there already?… It's really your seat, you know… the driver's seat…. but a part of you might have taken over that driver's seat… with or without your permission… If someone is sitting there now… politely ask them to get out of your driver's seat… and go back to their own seat in the bus… Now I am inviting you to sit down in the driver's seat… adjusting the rearview mirror… looking in that rearview mirror now… Who do you see there… on your bus?… Just noticing who is here… What they are wearing?… What do they look like?… Some of your Committee parts might be smiling and waving to you… Some of them might just be sitting there quietly… Others might be yelling… trying to get your attention… A few might be wearing masks… or be completely covered up because they don't want you to know them… yet…

Take a moment now to notice how you are feeling about being in the driver's seat of your Inner Committee's bus… just noticing how you feel… remembering that you are in charge… Whatever you are feeling is okay… Knowing that each of these passengers represents a part of yourself… and each one carries with it a special gift for you… They are each here to teach you something about yourself and your journey… Your job is only to watch.. and listen… and be curious…

Now, if you choose to… go ahead and turn the key in the ignition… putting the bus in gear… and driving…. simply driving your own bus… or maybe your bus has special powers and it can fly… just steering your bus forward… And there you are … you… in the driver's seat… If you aren't ready to drive your bus yet… you can choose to stay where you are… Give yourself permission to remain parked if you want to…

If you're driving… notice that there is a microphone attached to the dashboard… Go ahead and pick up the microphone… and make this announcement…
"Who would like to come up here and sit next to me in the passenger seat for a while?… Does anyone have anything to say to me right now about what's going on in my life?"… Then sit back… keep driving… and watch what happens…

Allowing one of your Committee members to come forward…
It might take a while… or someone might leap immediately into that seat beside you… Just allowing whatever happens next to be perfectly okay…

As you are driving… I invite you to spend a few minutes talking with this part of you who so graciously volunteered to step forward… asking what it wants to say to you… asking if it brings you a gift… asking if it needs anything from you right now… and then just listening… You don't have to do anything except drive your bus…

Now it's almost time to come back from this inner journey... so go ahead and drive... or fly... back to the spot where you first found your bus... parking the bus carefully... standing and bowing to the Committee member who was sitting in the passenger seat with you... thanking him or her for talking with you today... And then when you are ready... opening the door... climbing down the three steps... beginning your walk back to this class...

Following the sound of my voice back to this room... starting to feel your body resting on the chair... and your feet on the floor... taking a few deep breaths in and out to ground you back into this moment... stretching any part of your body that is needing to move... Coming back into your body as slowly as you need to...

Gently open your eyes when you are ready...
Take your time... I will wait for you... There is no rush...

.

The Conference Table

Begin by making yourself really comfortable for this next little while… Please listen to your body and respect what it is asking you for… so that you can relax and be at ease for this inner journey…

Now… focusing on your breath… feeling the air flowing in and out of your nostrils… in and out… in and out… Feeling your chest rising and falling with each breath… rising and falling… rising and falling… rising and falling…

Now you are even more relaxed… And in your imagination, I invite you to travel to your own personal inner sanctuary… a safe place that you are creating just for yourself… It might look and feel like somewhere you've already been… or it might be completely imaginary… Taking yourself there now… entering the building or the space… and just walking around for a bit… exploring… Noticing what you are seeing… any sounds… smells… and also noticing what you can touch… and what you are feeling…

As you are exploring… I invite you to start looking for a large table of some sort… It might be a kitchen table with a pretty tablecloth… or a picnic table outside… or a shiny mahogany conference table… It could be a big dining room table with a lace tablecloth and candles… or an altar… or a round table like they used in Camelot… Searching for any table at all… as long as it's large… Taking a few minutes to walk around your inner sanctuary looking for this table… and when you find it… go ahead and choose a seat… sit down and make yourself comfortable…

Now that you are sitting at this table… imagine the seats that are around it… The seats might be plain wooden chairs… or cushioned… folding chairs… benches… or even thrones… They might all look alike… or each one might be a different color or shape… Remembering that this is your journey and you can have whatever table… and whatever kind of seats you like…

You are sitting in the chair that is yours… and if you like… bring to mind an issue that you're dealing with in your life right now… It could be a physical issue… or something about a relationship… It might have something to do with your job or career… or maybe it's a concern about your lifestyle… or even about a big decision that you have to make…

Thinking about this for a moment… And now I invite you to imagine that there are a few people sitting in the seats that are around your table… Their faces aren't clear to you right now… You can think of them as your Committee that has come together to help you get some focus on this issue you are considering…

You can choose now to simply sit at the table with your Committee in silence… or share a meal together… or you can choose to ask this Committee what they think about your particular issue… promising them that you won't judge or criticize them… no matter what they say to you… Then listening… just listening carefully… to what each one has to say…

Some of your Committee parts might be supportive… Some of them might be saying critical things… Know that it's all okay… You don't need to talk back… You are just listening… becoming aware of your own inner self-talk…

You might not like some of the things that they say… In fact… one of these Committee members might seem intent on saying negative things to you… and that's okay… No matter what a particular Committee part says to you… I want you to say this to them… "Thank you for sharing"… and then move on to the next person on your Committee…

Taking a few minutes now to hold your space at the table… listening… listening carefully to what your committee has to say to you about this issue or concern that you've brought to them… Listening… and remembering that you are separate from them…

Remembering that you are in a safe place… a sacred sanctuary…
and you are always safe here…

Now it's almost time to begin leaving your inner sanctuary… I invite you to get up from your chair… See your committee members standing up as well… Now take a moment to look at each one… maybe make a little bow towards each of them… You might choose to say thank you as you bow… or something else…

Then in your own time… and in your own way…moving away from the table… walking out of your inner sanctuary the same way you entered it… and now following your special safe path… back… and back… until you are able to feel yourself sitting on this chair right now in this room…
following the sound of my voice back to our class today…

Becoming aware once again of your breath… You can feel the air coming into your body through your nose on each inhale… You can feel the air exiting your body through your mouth as you exhale… and you are noticing your chest rising and falling with each breath…

Coming back to your body…feeling your feet grounding you to the floor… and your legs against the chair you are in… You may want to lightly flex your fingers and toes… or gently shake out your arms and legs…

Opening your eyes when you feel ready…
Please take your time… I will wait for you…
Remembering that all is well…

Dancing with Your Inner Child

Taking a deep breath in… exhaling with a sound or a sigh… Again breathing in… and exhaling with a sigh… And one more time… in… and out… Now allowing your eyes to close gently… or keeping a soft downward gaze… giving your body and your mind permission to relax a little bit… and a little bit more… and to be comfortable… and at ease for these next several minutes…

Allowing your body to feel… really feel… the contact that it makes with the chair and with the floor… and adjusting your body in any way it needs to in order to be comfortable… and maybe even just a little bit more comfortable…

As you tune in to the rhythm of your breathing… imagine that when you inhale… you're inhaling a little bit of the sky… and it's very clear and very refreshing… And as you exhale, imagine that you're letting go of whatever you don't need right now… Inhaling the light, clear sky… Exhaling that which does not serve you right now…

Letting the rhythm of your breath be just what it is… a simple and beautiful process of taking in what's fresh and clear… and letting go of what's no longer needed…

Each breath you take relaxes and refreshes you… Your breathing and your mind are becoming clearer and clearer… Your body is relaxing a little bit more with each inhale and exhale…

Allowing your imagination to be open and receptive… still breathing in… and breathing out… You're going to take a short inner journey now… In your imagination… I invite you to put on your favorite jacket and walking shoes… Imagining yourself opening the door to your apartment or house and walking out… leaving the building you are in… closing the door gently behind you… Your home will be here for you… when you are ready to return…

Imagining yourself walking outside your home… and with the power of your imagination, you can bring yourself very quickly anywhere you want… so find yourself now… walking… walking… somewhere safe and beautiful… peaceful and quiet… You might be in the woods… or by the ocean… near a river… or a flower-filled meadow… and you are walking at whatever pace feels most comfortable to you in this moment…

Noticing the air around you… how it feels on your skin… Maybe you are deciding to go barefoot… Noticing the weather… Becoming aware of any sounds close to you or in the distance…

You are walking a bit more slowly now… It seems that you are looking for a small house or another dwelling place… You will know it when you see it… in your imagination…

When you come upon this dwelling place… spend a little time walking around it… and after a while… you are noticing that the front door is open… and a child is standing in the doorway… Stop for a moment and listen inside yourself… You might decide now to stay outside and simply wave to this child and then walk away… or you can choose to walk towards him or her… This is your inner child… If you are choosing to wave and walk away… go ahead and do that now… and then find a safe place to sit or lie down outside and take a nap… or have your own adventure…

If you are choosing to walk towards your inner child… keep walking until you are standing in front of him or her… Then… if it feels right… reach out and hold your little one's hands… You might want to stoop down… look into his or her eyes… saying, "I remember you!… I know you!"… Simply noticing how the child responds… And noticing everything about him or her… the hair… the eyes… the clothes… the shoes… and anything else you notice…

If it feels right to you… allow your inner child to bring you into their favorite room in this little house… Where is her or she taking you?…

As you enter this room with your inner child… you see a big comfortable rocking chair… And now you are walking over to the rocking chair… and sitting in it….. and if you choose to… only if you choose to… go ahead and invite this precious child onto your lap… Hold him or her… and rock for a while… How does it feel to be rocking your little one?…

After a while… you might want to ask your inner child if there's anything he or she needs from you… Just listening carefully… Paying attention…

Now… continuing to rock your little one… in this beautiful room… in this comfortable and safe little house you've found for your soul… rocking slowly… giving comfort… receiving comfort…

And… just for a moment… in your imagination…
see if you can switch places with the child…

Just for a moment… imagine that you are the little one who is being held…
and rocked… in the arms of a loving, adult being… slowly being rocked by this
loving grown-up… If you can, allow their big, unconditional love to wash over you…
You might be imagining that you are being held by an angel… or by your own
mother… or by an imaginary mother who only sees the good in you… who only
wants the best for you… whose only response to you is tender and loving…
Allowing yourself to bask in this for a few moments… Allowing yourself to be
a little child again… Allowing yourself to be held and cherished…

Listening as this beautiful being asks you what you need… What do you need?…
What are you saying to this one who loves you just as you are… to this one who rocks
you tenderly in this beautiful safe place?… Right now, just in this moment…
What do you need?… Still allowing yourself to be rocked gently… Gently rocking…

Now it's time to switch places again… Take your time…

You are now the loving adult who is rocking your own precious inner child…
You might want to kiss this child on the forehead… You might want to stroke
his or her hair… Find some way now to communicate how much you love them…
how much you will always love them…

It is time to start thinking about leaving… and if it feels right… ask your little one
to go with you… Maybe he or she says yes right away… Maybe there is some
hesitation… Just listening now to their response…

If your inner child has agreed… gently take their hand as you get up from the
rocking chair… Ask if they need to bring anything with them… and then begin
to retrace your steps slowly…

If your inner child does not want to come with you at this time… reassure them
that it's perfectly fine… Let them know that you will be there any time they call out
for you… Thank him or her for letting you visit with them today…
Then say good-bye… and begin to retrace your steps slowly…

Walking back out of the little house the way you came in…
Finding your way back home… back to the street that you live on…

back to the apartment building or house that is yours in the physical world… If you brought your little one back with you… remembering that he or she is in your care… Take a few moments to show them your home… Allow them to explore… noticing their delight to be sharing this time and this home with you…

Now just taking a few moments to focus on your breath… feeling your feet grounding you on the floor… your legs and your back against the chair… sensing into your shoulders… your neck… your head… paying attention to your breath… Bringing yourself fully back to your body… and to this room…

When you are ready… gently open your eyes…
Take all the time you need… I will wait for you… all is well.

Inner Queen

Begin by bringing your body into a comfortable position… relaxing your body… and relaxing your body a little bit more by moving however you need to… in order to adjust your body so that it is feeling ahhhhhh… just right… so comfortable… and a little bit more comfortable…

Closing your eyes if you feel comfortable doing so… or keeping a soft downward gaze… Coming to a gradual stillness… Bringing yourself to that place where you can hear your breath… Just listening to your breath for a moment… not trying to change it… just listening to it… Breath coming in… Breath going out… There is nowhere to go… and nothing to do right now… Just relaxing your body… Becoming calmer and more peaceful as you continue to bring your awareness to your breath… Calmer… calmer still… Peaceful… more peaceful still…

Breathing just a bit more slowly now… and setting the intention that during this inner journey today… you will be exploring this idea of yourself as a Queen… Queen of your own inner landscape… A kind, gracious queen who rules with compassion and fairness… Just setting the intention to be curious about this queenly part of you…

And now letting your thoughts drift… I invite you to use your imagination to take yourself to your own inner queendom… See yourself standing outside your castle… Where are you?… Examining your surroundings… the landscape… your castle… its foundation…

Now you are walking towards the main entrance of your castle… noticing as you walk how you are moving… Are you walking with a royal, queenly confidence?… If not, see if you can begin to change how you are walking…

And what are you wearing?… Royal clothing?… Is there a crown on your head?… If so, what is it made of?… How do you know that you are a queen?…

If you choose to… go ahead and enter your castle and spend a few minutes exploring… noticing the layout of the main floor… any passageways and doorways… choosing which doors to enter as you explore your royal castle…

Continuing to explore… Now imagine yourself saying…

"I am queen of my own castle… I rule over each incoming thought…
I rule over each outgoing message"… and just notice how you're feeling
as you say this… Keeping your royal presence shining forth… no matter
who or what you encounter in your castle…

Now wherever you are in your castle… you are taking yourself to your innermost secret chamber… only you know where this is… This is a special room designed especially for you… Spend a few minutes here… asking yourself… What is my heart longing for that I have not given myself?... What is my heart longing for that I have not given myself?... And sitting still as you await the answer… whatever answer is coming up for you… just listening for the answer…

Taking one last look at this secret innermost chamber that is yours and yours alone… knowing that you can return here whenever you choose to… And then slowly leave the chamber… following the path you used when you entered… and going back into the castle… Slowly finding your way back to the main entrance… and when you find it… leaving the castle… Maybe saying good-bye to any beings that you met here… and walking out of the castle now… away from the castle… your castle… and back up the path that led you in… which is now leading you out…

Slowly bringing yourself back to the sound of my voice...
taking a minute to stretch… to wiggle your fingers and toes…
coming fully back into your body however you need to…

Opening your eyes when you feel ready…
Take your time… I will wait for you…
Remember that all is well…

O Come All Ye Playful

Take a moment to get comfortable… Taking a slow breath in… and then slowly letting it out with a sigh… or any other kind of sound that your body wants to make… And again… breathing in… and letting it out with a sound… And one more time… in… out… and now letting your breath return to its own natural rhythm… easy… easy… There's nowhere to go… and nothing to do right now…
except be present with yourself… for yourself…

I invite you now to imagine that you are walking into your favorite movie theatre… or create a fantastical theatre in your imagination…

You find yourself stepping into this movie theatre now… looking around… seeking out the most comfortable seat that you can… settling in…. ahhh… Sinking into the seat… noticing the color… the texture… the feel of whatever it is you are sitting on… savoring the quiet of this special place… No one else is here right now… but you might choose to invite someone else to join you if that feels good to you… or just savor being alone… knowing you are completely safe… here in your imaginary movie theatre…

You notice that the lights are slowly dimming… and the movie screen is lighting up… You are seeing that the screen is showing a scene from your life today… whatever it was that you were doing right before you joined this class… See what you were doing… Smile at yourself, whatever it was… and now… simply notice that the film is rewinding… slowly… backwards in time… back to yesterday… to last week… last month…. last year… five years ago… and back and back in time… The film is rewinding more quickly now… and you might be a little bit curious about what the movie will show when it finally stops… It's still rewinding… rewinding back in time… back through the years of your life's journey…

Now the blurry motion of the rewinding is clearing… and you are seeing some scenes from your childhood… These are playful scenes… scenes of you… playing… Notice what you are seeing… what you are doing… how you are playing… if you are alone… or with others… or maybe you are seeing both kinds of play… What kind of play is it that is pleasurable to you here as a small child… that fully absorbs you… delights you?… What kind of play were you doing as a child that made you want to do it again and again?… And just noticing how this playfulness feels in your body… and how are you feeling as you play…

The movie is fast forwarding a bit now… and you are seeing yourself as an older child on the screen… but not yet a teenager… What are you doing?… How are you playing?… What kind of play is it that is pleasurable to you as an older child… that fully engages you… that is fun… that makes you lose all sense of time?… Maybe noticing also how this playfulness feels in your body… and how you are feeling as you play…

I'm going to be quiet for a few minutes… and I invite you to fast forward the movie screen to your adolescent years… and then see yourself as a young adult… then a more mature adult… moving the movie forward through your life at your own pace… stopping at scenes that show you playing in different ways… and I also invite you to continue to notice how these various forms of play make you feel in your body… and to be aware of how these forms of play made you feel in your heart…

I will tell you when you have one minute left…

So you have one more minute to review your relationship with play on the movie screen… Keep watching… keep noticing…

It's time to start thinking about leaving this imaginary movie theatre… But first… if you like… take a moment to bow to all of these playful memories… cherishing them… holding them close to your heart… And now fast forwarding your film… forward… and forward… right up to this present day… Seeing yourself on the movie screen sitting in your lovely movie theatre… Smiling at yourself… Smiling at this adventure you've just had… Turning off the projector…

Bringing yourself back to this time and place… back to this room we are in… Feeling your back and legs resting against the chair that supports you… Paying attention to your body right now and asking it what it needs to be more fully present and grounded… Maybe stretching your arms and legs… or just moving in some gentle way that feels good to your body which has been sitting for quite a while now…

Opening your eyes when you feel ready…
Please take your time… I will wait for you…
Remembering that all is well…

Taking the Inner Critic Out of the Director's Chair

Take a deep breath in… and out… and then gently allow your eyes to close… or keep a soft gaze downwards if that feels better to you today… Giving your body permission to relax… and then to relax just a little bit more… Giving your body and mind permission to be comfortable… comfortable… and relaxed… allowing your body to adjust itself in any way it needs to in order to be more relaxed… more comfortable…

As you tune in to the rhythm of your breath, imagine that when you inhale… you're inhaling a little bit of the sky… and it's very clear and very refreshing… And as you exhale, imagine that you're letting go of whatever you don't need right now… Inhaling the light, clear sky… Exhaling that which does not serve you right now…

Letting the rhythm of your breath be just what it is… a simple and beautiful process of taking in what's fresh and clear… and letting go of what's no longer needed…

Each breath you take relaxes and refreshes you… Your breath and your mind are becoming clearer and clearer… Your body is relaxing a little bit more with each inhale and exhale…

Each breath you take relaxes and refreshes you… Your breathing and your mind are becoming clearer and clearer… Your body is relaxing a little bit more with each inhale and exhale…

Now I invite you to imagine yourself driving a beautiful car…You decide what kind of car it is… and you are driving down a sunny California street… Palm trees are waving gently in the breeze… and you are feeling that all is right with your world… You are driving along… feeling safe and secure in your wonderful car… Feeling your body as it rests against the seat… No one is in the car but you… The radio is tuned to your favorite station… or maybe you've turned off the radio… Just listen… What do you hear as you drive along this beautiful California street?... What do you see?... What do you smell?...

Now you are approaching the parking lot of a large motion picture studio… You are driving into the parking lot… stopping at the security gate… and cheerfully telling the attendant your name… The attendant smiles and waves you in…

You are driving your car into the parking space closest to the main entrance of this movie studio… Noticing that in the center of this parking space is a large shiny golden star with your name inside it in glittery letters… How do you feel, seeing your name here like this… claiming that this priority parking space that is just for you?…

Taking your time as you get out of the car… closing the door… making your way into the big door of this movie studio… And when you get inside, you are noticing lots of people bustling around… You are realizing that you are on the set of a very important film… and the film that is being made is telling the story of your life… You are also realizing as you look around… that you are not only the star of the film… you are also its director…

I invite you now, if it feels right, to find your way across the set… to your very own director's chair… It's a special sturdy chair with an oak frame and canvas seat and back… Your name is embroidered on the back… You are approaching the chair from behind… admiring how your name looks there… See that now…

But… something isn't right… There is someone else sitting in your director's chair… You move a little closer and see that your Inner Critic is occupying your director's chair… and not only that, he or she is actually directing your film…

Just watch your Inner Critic for a moment… and pay attention to what part of your life is being filmed right now… Noticing carefully how your Inner Critic is directing this part of your life… What is this Critic saying about this part of your life?… How does he or she think this part of your life should look?…

And now… remembering that your Inner Critic is just one of your many inner parts… remembering that your Inner Critic is not you… remembering that this director's chair really does belong to you and no one else… I invite you to say… in your loudest, best director's voice… "Stop Action!"… And simply watch as the acting and the filming stop… watching as all the actors and film crew turn to you to see what you want them to do next… noticing that they are waiting for direction from you…

You might decide now to give them all a break… If so, tell them to "take ten" or something like that… and watch as they all move away from you now… to other parts of the set… so they can have their break… Now if it feels right, go ahead and take a few steps closer to your Inner Critic… your Inner Critic who still happens to be sitting in your director's chair… Saying hello to him or her… Getting a closer look… If you want, introduce yourself… Smile… Everything really is okay… You are in control of

this inner journey that you're on... Shake his or her hand if you feel like it...
If it feels okay to you... ask your Inner Critic why he or she is sitting in your director's chair... And listen, just listen to the answer...

You might want to ask what your Inner Critic is afraid might happen... if he or she were to get out of the director's seat and leave the set... and again, just listen to the response... It's okay to just listen... There's no need to respond...

today... for being honest with you... And then, if you feel like you want to do this... Tell him or her that you are the real director of this movie about your life... and that it's time for you to sit in the director's chair again... Watch as your Inner Critic gets up from the chair and leaves the set... Notice how it feels for you to sit in the director's chair again... as the cast and crew come back to the set and the filming begins again... Maybe noticing how you feel now that your Inner Critic has left the set... What is it like to actually be the one in charge of this movie...this film that is your life?... And how are you directing this part of your life differently now that you are in control again?...

Just getting a sense of being the director of your own life again... and enjoying how that feels for a little while...

It's almost time to leave now... It's the end of the day and everyone is getting ready to go home for the night... You find yourself saying good-bye to everyone on the set for now... the actors... the camera operators... your assistants... Thanking them all for being part of your movie... And now you are finding your way back to your beautiful car... Starting the engine... Taking the wheel... Waving goodbye to the smiling attendant at the gate... Noticing how good it feels to be driving your own car again... Strong and in control... Driving back through the streets that brought you to the movie studio... Driving with confidence and ease...

And when you are ready... bringing yourself back to this room that we are in together... Noticing your breath once again... following the sound of my voice right back here... Slowly becoming aware of your body... maybe shifting a little in your seat... Noticing your feet on the floor grounding you more and more into your body... Moving gently in some way that brings you back into the present moment a bit more...

And opening your eyes gently when you feel ready... No need to hurry...
I will wait for you... All is well.

The Great White Feather

When you are ready, allow your eyes to gently close… or keep a soft downward gaze… Bringing yourself to stillness… Giving yourself permission to slow down… to relax your body… and your mind… for this next little while… Just giving yourself permission to come home to Spirit… to the One that holds the many parts of your world… Paying attention to your breath… Not trying to change it… Just noticing as you breathe in… and noticing as you breathe out… There is nowhere to go for now… and there is nothing to do but sit still with yourself and listen inside… relaxing… and now relaxing just a little bit more…

In your imagination now… I invite you to remember the last time you behaved in a way that was contrary to your best, brightest, most authentic self… Maybe you said something that was hurtful… Perhaps you engaged in an addictive behavior… or did something that got in the way of one of your goals… Whatever it was, just call it to mind now… remembering… what you said… or did… how you felt… in your body… in your mind… Remembering too… if you said anything to yourself afterwards that made you feel even worse about yourself… Maybe remembering how hard it was to forgive yourself… Perhaps you were "beating yourself up"… for making this mistake… for acting in this way…

I invite now… as you are remembering this situation… to become aware that someone is coming towards you… a beautiful being of light… Take a moment to notice who this is… A being of light… What does this being look like?… Are there any colors… sounds… fragrances… arising… as he or she approaches you?…

And you find yourself smiling a bit… relaxing your shoulders… He or she is carrying a large white feather… The white feather is about half the size of your body… The being of light gently hands you this large shimmering white feather instead… He or she says to you… "If you have to beat yourself up, dear one… please use this instead"…

So go ahead now… Start tapping yourself on the head and face… and on your arms and legs… with this soft white feather… Notice how this feels… You might be finding that you cannot do this without smiling… Maybe you're even laughing because it tickles…

Taking a moment now to thank the Being of Light who gave you the large white feather… and ask if you can bring the feather back with you…

knowing that you can visit this being any time you want to…
simply by closing your eyes and taking a breath…

Now when you are ready… and only when you are ready… take another moment to come back to your body… and to your breath… paying close attention to how your body feels right now… breathing a little more deeply and consciously now… following the sound of my voice back to this present moment… back to this day and time…

If it feels good to do so, stretch your fingers and toes… or move your body in some way that feels grounding to you… You might at this time choose to offer a prayer of thanksgiving to Spirit… for this time of stillness… for the gift of your imagination… and for this gentle reminder of how to be kinder to yourself…

Opening your eyes gently when you are ready… taking your time…
I will wait for you… All is well…

Offering Comfort to a Hurting Committee Part

I invite you to find a way to make yourself comfortable for the next several minutes… Settling in to your body… Resting your body… There's nowhere to go… and nothing to do right now… Resting… Relaxing… Settling in to your mind as well… Noticing thoughts as they come and go… just noticing… Resting your mind from worries or fears for this little while… and settling in to your spirit… whatever that means to you… Resting… Relaxing… Feeling a little calmer now… and more relaxed with every breath…

In your imagination, I invite you to take yourself to a safe, beautiful place… a sanctuary… an inner sanctuary… It might be a place you have been in your life on the earthly plane… or somewhere purely of your imagination… Take yourself gently there now… outside or inside… Find a place to sit or stand very still here… so that all of your senses can absorb the pure beauty and safety of this place… Seeing… Listening… Smelling… Touching… Maybe even tasting… Noticing also how it feels to be here… in this safe sanctuary space today…

If it feels right to you… bring to mind the inner part of you who is hurting today… and invite this part to join you in this space… Maybe saying hello… What does he or she look like?... What is this part wearing?... You might want to try bowing to this part… acknowledging its presence in your life… Thanking it for being willing to speak its truth to you… And then stepping back… several paces away from your hurting part…

Activating Witness energy now …. and listening with compassion for a moment as this part of you does speak its truth about what it is thinking… and what it is feeling… Allowing it to be fully expressive… Reminding it and yourself that you are in a safe place for healing… Remembering that this is just one part of you… This is not your only part… Allowing this part to have its loneliness… or its sadness… its fear… or its anger… or whatever it is feeling… Just allowing it to be okay… Becoming aware that you don't need to dissolve into this feeling yourself… The bigger you is a compassionate witness now… and this hurting part is a part of you… but it is not all of you…

Now… watching as this part lapses into silence again… And if you like, calling into this sanctuary one of your Community members… Is there a friend… a family member… a personal pet… or a teacher… who would like to offer something to this part who is hurting today?... Go ahead and invite this Community member to join your hurting part now… And you are just watching… from several steps away…

whatever is happening… How is this person or pet comforting your hurting part?… What words or thoughts are being communicated?… You are simply witnessing… watching… allowing the comfort to be given… and received…

If it feels right to you… go ahead and invite this Community member to step back and stand with you… several paces away from the hurting part… Together call in a Council member… This might be an archetypal energy or a spirit guide… Maybe even some form of the goddess… Just imagine now calling in a balanced energy with some higher wisdom to share with your hurting part… And then observe with compassion… How does this higher guide assist your hurting part?… What wisdom does it speak or share?… And you are simply witnessing… allowing the wisdom to be communicated… and received…

Now invite this Council guide to step back… and stand with you and your Community member… Several paces away from the hurting part… And together call in one of your Animal Companions to offer whatever this hurting part is most in need of right now… Watch kindly as the Animal Guide comes forward towards your hurting part… How does it comfort?… What guidance does it offer?…
And you are simply watching with compassion… witnessing…
allowing the guidance to be offered… and received…

You and your Council Guide and your Community member are all moving forward now to join this Animal Companion… and all of you are forming a small circle around your hurting part… You might be holding hands… or paws or wings… or you might simply be standing with hands or paws or wings over your hearts…

As you are standing in this circle of protection around your hurting part… you are becoming aware of Source… whatever you choose to call Source… becoming aware of The One who holds the many parts of your journey… becoming aware of The One from which you came… and from which all these beings came… Knowing that none of you are alone… that you are all connected…. and as you in this circle are connected to one another, so you are connected to all sentient beings… and all that comes from Source… Feeling that connection now… however it manifests to you… savoring it… immersing yourself in it… feeling yourself supported and surrounded and loved by it…

Very good… I invite you now… if it feels right… to ask the hurting part how it is feeling now… Giving it some space and time to share… Asking it if it has anything to

share with this Circle that has come to bring it comfort and solace today…
and again… just listening… with kindness and compassion…

Finding a way to reassure this hurting part that it is not alone… and that it has a right to feel whatever it is feeling… Maybe inviting it to ask you for help if its feelings ever are overwhelming again… Reminding him or her that you are always available for comfort and reassurance… as are the others who have joined you in the circle today…

In some way that feels good… I invite you to express gratitude to your Community member… your Council Guide… and your Animal Companion… for helping you today with your hurting part… Then waving good-bye or maybe even blowing them kisses as they walk slowly away…

And now… if your hurting part seems willing… take his or her hand… and find your way slowly… slowly… back to this class… Following the sound of my voice away from this special sanctuary you've been in… Knowing that you can return here any time you like… simply by taking a breath…

Continuing to hold the hurting part in your heart… find a gentle way to land back here in your body… Noticing your feet grounding yourself to the earth… the sensation of your back and legs against the chair… Maybe moving your body in some gentle way… stretching…

Opening your eyes when you feel ready…. Taking your time…
I will wait for you… Remembering that all is well…

Part 4

Community

Truth is a matter of the imagination.

~ Ursula K. LeGuin

Indra's Net

Begin by making yourself as comfortable as you can… Please listen to your body and respect whatever it is asking for in this moment… Making any adjustments you need to make in order to allow yourself to relax a little bit more… and a little bit more… Shifting any parts of your body that will help you let go of any tension you are holding… so that you can relax… even a bit more…

I invite you to close your eyes whenever you feel ready to do so… or simply keep a soft downward gaze… And now try focusing on your breath for a moment… Feeling the air flowing in and out of your nose… in and out… in and out… Feeling your chest rising and falling with each breath… rising and falling… rising and falling… rising and falling…

Now that you are feeling even more comfortable… and even a little more relaxed… I invite you to see in your imagination a very wide net… something like a fishing net… And imagine that we are all holding onto the edge of this net… You are slowly watching as the net grows larger and larger… It is expanding past the walls of this room we are in… past this building… It is slowly becoming bigger and wider… It is stretching throughout all of this city now… and beyond this city to our entire continent… It is slowly unfolding to embrace the whole earth…
Seeing this net in your mind's eye if you can… encircling the world…

Breathing in deeply… focusing on the feel of the net in your hands right now… knowing that you are connected to everyone here in some way…You are connected to everyone in this town… this state… this country… the world… You are a part of the net that weaves us all together… Just noticing how this feels… this knowing that you are so connected…

Now… imagine that each intersection of the net contains a brilliant jewel…
What kind of jewels do you see?… Are they all the same, or is each one different?… It doesn't matter… Just picture it how you would like it to be… You are looking closely at one of the jewels in the net now… It is brilliant and seems to be lit from within… It is so brilliant that it is reflecting all of the other jewels in its bright surface…
All of the jewels of this net are like this… and you are noticing how each one shimmers and reflects the light from all the other jewels…

As you are looking at the beautiful jewels that make up this infinite net…

I invite you to find the jewel that represents one of your beloved Community members… Find the jewel that belongs to that person… Even if they are no longer with us… they are still a part of this net… They are still connected to you… to us… because the net is what holds us all together in this life… and beyond this life… So go ahead and find their jewel… and notice how it shines… Notice how their jewel is different from all the other jewels… What makes it special?... What makes it priceless to you?...

If you'd like to say something to that person or pet… do so now in your imagination… and know that they can hear you… Listen for a few moments… Notice if they respond to you in any way…

It's time to start thinking about coming back to this room now… But before you do… Take a moment to thank all the jewels of the net… and particularly the Community member whose jewel you connected with today… Knowing that you can come back to this net any time you need to… just by closing your eyes and taking a breath…

Take one last look at the infinite, shimmering net… and remember that you are a part of it… that you will always be a part of it.. that we are all connected and held by it… And now… making the journey back to this time and place… Taking your time… Feeling your feet solidly on the floor beneath you… Noticing how your body feels against your chair… Breathing in and out at your own pace… as you return to the sound of my voice… as you return to this moment in time…

And when you feel yourself fully present here again…
Gently open your eyes… Take your time… I will wait for you…
Remembering that all is well…

Blessed Community Circle

Begin by making yourself as comfortable as you can… Listen to your body… Respect what it is asking you for right now… Adjusting or shifting your body in any way that gives you that feeling of ahhhh… Now giving your body permission to relax a little bit… and maybe even a little bit more…

Focusing on your breath… Feeling the air flowing in and out of your nose… in and out… in and out… Feeling your chest rising and falling with each breath… Rising and falling… Rising and falling… Rising and falling…

Breathing in light… and goodness… and love… Breathing out any tension or worry or thoughts that are getting in the way of your being present right here… right now… in this moment with yourself… Breathing in light… Breathing out tension… Breathing in light… Breathing out tension…

Now you are even more relaxed… and in your imagination I invite you to find yourself walking outdoors… somewhere safe and precious to you… You are walking towards a building that has sweet memories for you… Maybe it's the house where you grew up… It might be the house you live in now… or another building or home or place… where you felt or feel absolutely safe and loved…

See yourself now walking into this place of love and goodness… There is a very large space in this building… Find yourself in this space now… You are standing in the center of it… Noticing the colors on the walls… the floors… … the furniture… Are you hearing any sounds?... And also… noticing how you are feeling…

Now… standing in the center of this very large room or space… you notice that other people are entering the room… Slowly they are coming in to join you… They are forming a large circle all around you… This is your Blessed Community Circle… Here in this circle are all of the sentient beings who form your true Community…

Take a look around you now… as they continue to enter and form a large circle all around you… Who is here with you today?... See their faces… Notice how wonderful it is to have them all in this same space with you… all of them… Noticing that there may be people here from your past…

People who have died and passed on to the other side…

People who are a part of your life now…

Pets who have loved you unconditionally…both past and present…

Noticing too that there are people here whom you've never met… people you are drawn to… people who have touched your life through their art… or words… religion… politics… or teaching…

Each of these beings is part of your own Blessed Community Circle…
And all have come here together today to celebrate you!…

You are still standing in the center of this Circle… and I invite you to just imagine that each person and animal who is here… is shining its precious light onto you in the center… all at once… And now you are turning… turning slowly around… so you can look into the eyes of each and every one… Just savoring the feeling of love and light that washes over you as you do this… And also… if you choose… imagine a greater, Divine Love… shining down on all of you from above… and filling you with a feeling of safety and of being loved…

Now if it feels right… you might want to ask your Circle if someone has a message for you right now… in your life… Inviting one of them to join you in the center… and then just listening to the message that this being has to give you today…

It's time now to start to think about coming back to our workshop… but first… find a way to say good-bye to your Blessed Community Circle… reminding yourself that you will be back soon… knowing that you can be here in this loving space… connected with your Community… anytime… in just a matter of seconds… simply by closing your eyes and taking a breath…

And when you are ready… slowly and mindfully leave the Circle… finding your way back through the building the same way you came in… walking slowly and easily… back down the sacred path…

Becoming aware of the breath flowing in and out of your nose… becoming mindful of the love that you are bringing back with you… love… and a new sense of connection to your own blessed community…

And then in your own time and your own way… bringing yourself back to this room… to this time and place… Feeling your feet resting on the floor… Sensing your legs and your back against the chair… Becoming aware of your body now… and gently shifting or stretching or moving your body in a way that feels really good…

Then in your own time… gently opening your eyes…
Taking your time… I will wait for you… All is well…

Loving-Kindness (Metta)

When you are ready, allow your eyes to gently close… or simply keep a soft downward gaze… bringing your body and your mind to a deliberate centered stillness… Giving yourself permission to relax… paying attention to your breath… Breathing in the stillness that is always inside of you… breathing out any inner chaos… Breathing in peace… and breathe out any thoughts that might be getting in the way of that peace… Giving yourself permission to just breathe in… to just breathe out… and to simply relax a little bit more…

This Metta Meditation is very simple… In the first part, we direct the energy of lovingkindness towards ourselves… Try saying these words to yourself… and as you say the words… imagine the warmth of your heart radiating towards all parts of your own being… May I be safe… May I be happy… May I be healthy… May I be free… And again… May I be safe… May I be happy… May I be healthy… May I be free…

In the second part, we direct the energy of lovingkindness towards someone we love… So just imagine this loved one sitting across from you now… I am going to use the pronoun "she" as I lead us through this part… but feel free to substitute your loved one's first name if you like… May she be safe… May she be happy… May she be healthy… May she be free… And again… May she be safe… May she be happy… May she be healthy… May she be free…

In the third part, we direct the energy of lovingkindness towards someone we don't know… someone we feel neutral towards… Perhaps it's someone ahead of us in line at the grocery store… or our mail carrier… or the cashier at the coffee shop… Picture someone like this in your mind's eye now… and begin… May he be safe… May he be happy… May he be healthy… May he be free… And again… May he be safe… May he be happy… May he be healthy… May he be free…

In the next part, we direct this powerful energy of lovingkindness towards someone who causes us difficulty… or someone with whom we experience conflict… So imagine this person sitting across from you… and don't worry… you are not going to engage in conversation or argument with them… I am going to use the pronoun "she" as I lead us through this part… but you might find it more powerful to use his or her first name instead… May she be safe… May she be happy… May she be healthy… May she be free… This might be difficult… Just remind yourself that it's all okay…

and remember to breathe… Let's try it one more time now… May she be safe…
May she be happy… May she be healthy… May she be free…

In the last part of Metta practice, we direct the energy of lovingkindness towards all sentient beings… Breathing in and out… slowly… May all beings be safe… May all beings be happy… May all beings be healthy… May all beings be free… And again… May all beings be safe… May all beings be happy… May all beings be healthy… May all beings be free…

Before we come back… take a moment to bow to yourself… and to your loved one… and to the neutral person… to the person with whom you are in conflict… to all sentient beings… and finally, once again… to yourself…

Now I invite you to come back to your body… Feeling all the parts of your body against your chair or your bed… Following the sound of my voice back to this present moment… Moving or stretching your body in any way that feels good to you… Very good…

Opening your eyes when you are ready… Taking your time…
I will wait for you… All is well…

Part 5

Archetypes

*Without this playing with fantasy,
no creative work has ever come to birth.
The debt we owe to the play of imagination
is incalculable.*

~ Carl Jung

Meeting a Council Guide

Begin by taking a deep breath through your nose and hold it for a few seconds… and then let it out through your mouth with a sigh or another sound… Again, inhale though your nose… and let go of the breath with a relaxing sigh or sound… Do this a few times… and each time… let the relaxation that you are beginning to feel… grow a little deeper… Closing your eyes if it feels comfortable to do so… or keeping a soft downward gaze…

Now see if you can use your mind to scan your body for tension… Starting at the top of your head and slowly working down to the soles of your feet… Noticing wherever your muscles are holding on… If you are feeling tightness anywhere… you might want to invite in looseness and softness… There is nowhere to go and nothing to do for the next several minutes… Relaxing just a little bit more… as much as you can for now…

Your body is settling into a more comfortable position… with no holding on… no grasping… Your breath is becoming a little bit calmer… a bit more relaxed… a little bit calmer… a bit more relaxed…

I invite you now to imagine that you are in a beautiful place… This is a special place that you can go to in your imagination to find peace and solitude… See yourself in this place… this sanctuary that is yours and yours alone…

Imagining now that it is a beautiful day here… wherever you are in your imagination… What does the sky look like?... How does the air feel on your skin?... Take a moment to listen all around you… What can you hear?... Are there any fragrances wafting their way to you?...

When you are ready… in your imagination… I invite you to look for a path that leads away from the spot where you have been exploring… If you choose to, begin walking on this path… You are sensing that this path will take you to another place… also a peaceful place… but this will be a place where you will meet a being of great wisdom and love… Following this path now… until it comes to a large open space…

You are seeing this place as sacred and holy somehow… What do you notice in this area that makes you feel that Divine energy is present?... Are there sacred objects?... Do you hear sacred music?... Just looking around and noticing everything about this peaceful, sacred, welcoming space…

Finding a seat now… go ahead and imagine now that you are inviting into this wonderful place… a being of great wisdom and compassion… Because you seek understanding… this being is pleased to come to you… Soon you find that seated across from you is someone whose heart is full of love… and whose mind is pure and wise… As you are looking into their eyes… you are seeing only love… It is as if their whole body is radiating light and love to you…

From the area of this being's heart… a bright light shines… directly into your heart… You are feeling in that light a warm and special energy… A sense of well-being is building in your heart… spreading through your whole body… From head to toe… you are filling with a loving light that is flowing into every cell of your body… Every cell… every molecule in your body… is being touched by this love…

Now… listening inside yourself… perhaps you find that you have a question for this wise one… Perhaps something has been troubling you and you would like some guidance… Feel free now to ask whatever you would like of this wise being… Form your question… and then listen very carefully… Take as much time as you need… Knowing that the answer may come as a thought… or you might hear words in your mind… or the wise being might show you an image… Just savoring this gift of inner time… and opening to whatever arises from this being of wisdom who has come to be with you today…

You might also choose to have a dialogue with this friendly being…
or maybe the two of you will just sit quietly together… Do whatever feels right for you…

And now it is time to start thinking about leaving this sacred clearing and this wise being… but before you leave… find some way to say good-bye to this loving one who has come here to be with you… and know that you can return at any time… simply by closing your eyes and taking a breath… Knowing also that this loving being is always with you… whether you are consciously aware of it or not…

Walking back down the path… away from the clearing… and standing once again in the warm light of the sun… in the beautiful place where you first arrived…

And when you are ready… bringing yourself back to this day and this time…
back to this room that we are in together… Focusing on your breath again… Following the sound of my voice right back here… Coming back slowly…
Becoming aware of your body… Maybe shifting a little bit in your seat…
Noticing your feet on the floor grounding you more and more into your body… Moving gently in some way that **brings** you back into your body a bit more…

Opening your eyes gently when you feel ready… No need to hurry…
I will wait for you… All is well…

Meeting Your Creative Muse

Please begin by making yourself comfortable… Sitting as straight as you can… Allowing your chair to support your whole body… Listening to your body… Respect what it is asking you for right now… and shifting or adjusting any body parts so that you can be a bit more relaxed… and maybe even a bit more relaxed…

Now focusing on your breath… feeling the air flowing in and out of your nose… in and out… in and out… Feel your chest rising and falling with each breath… rising and falling… rising and falling… Breathing in… breathing out… Breathing in… breathing out…

Every time you breathe in… imagine that you are breathing in the warm, sweet air of creativity that is all around you at this moment… And every time you breathe out imagine breathing out any worries or stress… Breathing in creativity… breathing out worries… Breathing in creativity… breathing out stress… Slowing down your breath just a little bit… Slowing down your thoughts a little bit more… Relaxing… Relaxing… Being so… so… gentle with yourself…

And when all is quiet and calm within… I invite you to take yourself… in your imagination… to a hot, dry desert… All is quiet here… You can see the sun shimmering on the sand… Your skin feels warm in the heat of this beautiful golden sun… In the distance you might be able to see a circle of tall flowering cactus plants… If it feels right, head on over to them now… Taking your time… If you are thirsty, notice that you are wearing a magical fanny pack and there is a water bottle inside that will never be empty… so drink some water if you need that… and continue walking towards the circle of cacti…

As you get closer… you notice that they are flowering with the most beautiful and fragrant flowers… What color are these flowers?… You might want to pick one and weave it into your hair… or place it in a buttonhole… or maybe you'll choose to leave the flowers where they are and just inhale their fragrance for a moment…

Now you are standing in the center of this circle of tall blossoming cactus plants… Some of them are as big as trees… You can choose to be here alone if you want… or you can choose to invite some creative people to join you… If you want to, imagine several different creative people standing around you in the circle of cacti… Make eye contact with each one… Feel their creative energy beaming into you… Maybe smiling… Laughing… Maybe even dancing if that feels good… Knowing that this is a time of celebration of your creativity as well… Because you recognize the creative spirit in each of them… you can acknowledge that you too possess it…

After a while… you notice that there is a large metal circle in the sand… If you choose to, get down on your hands and knees… and touch this metal circle… Brush some of the sand off of it… You can see that there is a handle on this metal circle… If it feels right… just pull gently on the handle until the metal circle easily lifts up in your hands… You are opening the door…

If you feel curious… dip your head into the opening in the sand… You can hear music coming from deep within the earth… You can see beautiful lights down below… and it smells like a lovely mixture of all of your favorite fragrances…

You raise your head back up into the bright desert sunshine… and look around at your creative companions… They are urging you to go down through the opening… to explore what is beneath the surface… "We have been there"… they are saying… You hear the words… "safe"… "joy"… and "self-expression"… What other words are you hearing as they encourage you to go deeper?…

Looking back down into the earth… you see someone or something below you… It is holding the bottom of a beautiful shimmering ladder… If you want to… only if you choose to… climb down the ladder… down… down… If you want to stay up in the desert sun and play with your creative friends for these next few minutes… that's okay too… Feel free to make the choice that is best for you… in this moment…

If you are journeying down… keep climbing slowly down the silver ladder… and when you get to the bottom… notice who has been there holding the ladder steady for you… It might be a person… someone you know or don't know… It could be a mythic creature or a spirit guide… Or maybe it's an angel… or even a special animal friend… Whoever it is… this is your Creative Muse for today… If you want, shake his or her hand… or paw or wing… and allow your Muse to take you on a little tour of your own creative depths…

During your tour, make note of what you see… and hear… and smell… and touch… What creative adventures lie hidden below the surface for you… in your own inner world today?…

After a while…your Creative Muse guides you to a large open area where there is a bonfire burning… Sit next to the fire for a while with your Muse… resting in the presence of this creative spirit… If you have questions for him or her… now is a good time to ask… and simply listen for any answers that you are given…

In a little while… you're going to be finding your way back to the ladder…
but first… take a moment… and think about something that has been getting in the way of your own creative playtime back on the surface of your life… Think of those times when you long for creative time but don't give it to yourself…
What is it that is stopping you?…

Your Creative Muse is handing you a piece of paper and a pen… Go ahead and write whatever it is that blocks you from your joyful creativity… Write it down on the piece of paper… and then toss it into the bonfire… and watch it disintegrate to ashes before your eyes… You might be noticing that you feel freer… calmer… or that something has been released from inside of you… and it feels good to know that you did it yourself…

Now it is time to find your way back to the ladder… Your Creative Muse is guiding you back to the opening where you entered this creative space… So say good-bye to him or her now… Be sure to express gratitude for their willingness to guide you today… taking all the time you need… and when you are ready… you can climb back up the ladder… up and up and up… knowing that your Creative Muse is holding the ladder steady for you and that you will not fall…

When you reach the top… climb joyfully back into the desert sunshine… Your creative team is still here waiting for you… cheering you on… You might want to return later and toss around some ideas with one or all of them…

Now… thanking each of them for joining you today… You might want to hug them or shake their hands… or just look each of them in the eyes… but do take a moment to bask in their creative energy… Take a moment now to appreciate the creative blessings they have gifted you with on your journey…

And when you are ready… you can leave the circle of flowering cacti in the warm and sandy desert… knowing that you can return here any time you like simply by closing your eyes and taking a breath… And find your way slowly… slowly back… to this room… following the sound of my voice… back here to this time and this place…

Finding a gentle way now to bring yourself back into your physical body… Feeling your feet on the floor… noticing the position your legs are in… feeling your back against the chair… Maybe slowly moving your head from side to side… or shaking out your hands… Finding a way to ground yourself back into your physical body…

When you are ready, open your eyes… There is no rush… I will wait for you… Take your time… Knowing that all is well…

Archetypes Along Your Journey

Please begin by making yourself comfortable… Sitting as straight as you can… Allowing your chair to support your whole body… Listening to your body… Respecting what it is asking for right now… and shifting or adjusting in any way so that you can be a bit more relaxed… and even a bit more relaxed than that…

Now focusing on your breathing… Feeling the air flowing in and out of your nose… in and out… in and out… Feel your chest rising and falling with each breath… rising and falling… rising and falling… Breathing in… breathing out… Breathing in… breathing out…

Every time you breathe in… imagine that you are breathing in the sweet air of wisdom that is all around you at this moment… Every time you breathe out… imagine that you are breathing out any worries or stress… Breathing in wisdom… breathing out worries… Breathing in wisdom… breathing out stress… Slowing down your breath just a little bit if you can… Also slowing down your thoughts just a little bit more… Relaxing… relaxing… being so… so… gentle with yourself…

And when all is quiet and calm within… I invite you to take yourself… in your imagination… to a large open meadow or field… The sky here is wide… and as blue as you want it to be… You can't see anything or anyone for miles and miles…. But you don't feel alone… You are feeling safe here… in this wide open space… Noticing the sun on your skin… Noticing the silence… the peace… or any sounds in the distance…

This place where you are standing represents where you are on your life's path right now… So now that you know this… use your imagination to fill in the scenery a little bit… You might be in a really creative phase of your life, so there might be beautiful waterfalls and lots of green foliage and flowers… Or you might be in a difficult part of your life's path, so the space might be rocky or even mountainous… Perhaps you are feeling that your life is like a dried up desert… or a jungle… or something else entirely… How does where you are on your life journey right now look to you… in this space that is yours and yours alone?… And what about the air… Is it clear… foggy?… polluted?… sweet?… There are no right answers… It is simply what it is… nothing more, nothing less… And you are just observing… just noticing… not trying to change it… simply noticing your current location…

Noticing colors… sounds… smells… textures… Maybe even noticing how your body feels in this place that gives image to where you stand on your life's journey at this time… Are you breathless from climbing… tingly from joy… tired from the journey… just how does your body feel to be in this landscape of your place on your life journey?…

Now I invite you to take a look around… until you find a magical vehicle that is going to lift you effortlessly into the air to give you some perspective on your life's journey at this time… It might be a balloon… or a rainbow colored airplane… a magic carpet… a silly looking flying machine… or maybe you will suddenly be given wings to fly… Just take a moment to look around… until you find this magic vehicle… Now you are climbing in or on it… and then… slowly… slowly… allow it to lift you up… up… into the sky… Lifting you up a little farther… until you are hovering about 100 feet above the landscape of your current life journey… or whatever feels a comfortable distance to you… Remembering that this vehicle is magical… and you are safe… completely and totally safe at all times… Remembering too that you are the one who is in control of this journey at all times…

Now… still hovering in one place… try looking down towards the landscape of your current location… and notice that… from this high up… it is just one little spot on a very long path or roadway… Looking towards the left and noticing the path that led to where you are right now on your journey… Now looking towards the right and noticing how the road continues on… What you are seeing now is the aerial view of your life's journey… And you are noticing how… all along the path… at various places… there are certain Beings of Light hovering over your path…

They might appear as physical entities… or they might look like glowing spaces… or beautiful multicolored lights… These Beings of Light are representing the archetypes that have been present to you as guides on your life's journey… These are the archetypal energies who are currently guiding you… and those who will be with you as your journey continues… You are high enough now to see all of it… your whole life's journey… unfolding below…

If you choose… still floating high in the air… turn your magical flying vehicle to the left and steer yourself away from your current location… still flying now… and travel to where the path of your life began…

When you arrive at the beginning of your life's path… bring your magical vehicle a little bit lower… Note the year where your path begins… and also note that because you are a little bit closer to the ground… you can see your entire childhood from up this high... And because you are closer... you can also see more clearly the specific guiding archetypes or themes that have shaped your life and your path... Making note of these themes or archetypes now... as you are looking down over your infant and childhood years... What were you doing?... What were you passionate about at that time of your life?... Just drifting slowly overhead... and noticing... Not judging or criticizing or wishing it was different... Just noticing... and allowing the archetypal energies to make themselves clearer to you... Perhaps becoming aware of any themes or patterns that emerged during your childhood years...

And now... steering your magical flying machine further on the path... You are now hovering over your adolescent years... As you look down over these teenage years... simply notice... What were you doing?... What were you passionate about at that time of your life?... Just drifting slowly overhead... and noticing... Not judging or criticizing... just noticing... and allowing any archetypal energies to make themselves clearer to you... Noticing any themes or patterns from your childhood years that continued on with you to adolescence... Maybe noticing any themes or patterns that emerged and were new to you during your adolescent years...

Very good... Now steering your magical flying machine onward to the right... following your life's path... slowly... Looking down on the different stages of your life... One set of years at a time... What were you passionate about then?... What were you doing?... Just drifting slowly overhead... and noticing... Not judging or criticizing... just noticing... and allowing the archetypal energies... those beings of light... to make themselves clearer to you... Noticing if you are seeing any themes or patterns emerge... I will give you a few minutes now... to observe the other stages of your life... in your own time... taking your time...

I invite you now to bring yourself in your flying machine back to the current landscape of your journey... Still hovering overhead... Still feeling safe and secure... Perhaps being more aware of the big picture of your life... the overview of your own particular path...

And looking down on your current location... Noticing what archetypal energies or themes are present for you right now in your life... with whatever's going on for you now... And also noticing which of them have traveled with you from the beginning of your journey... and which of them are brand new... emerging only now...

Now looking towards the right... where the path of your journey continues... hovering in your flying machine right where you are... just looking ahead on your journey... What guides can you see that might be already there ahead of you... waiting to guide you on your journey?...

And just noticing... how does it feel... looking ahead like this... to know that you will not be traveling alone... that these archetypal guides and energies "have your back" so to speak... all along the way?... Noticing how you feel in your body... and in your heart... as you remember that you are guided and watched over and loved... from near as well as from afar...

Now steering your magical vehicle down... slowly down and down... until you land right back in the middle of your current landscape... whatever that is for you... Stepping out of your vehicle... or shedding your wings... and bowing with gratitude... to the vehicle... to the wings... to the Beings of Light... to the archetypes... for taking you on this magical journey today...

And then turning all the way around slowly... as you watch your current landscape magically and slowly disappear... until you are standing in the wide open, clear meadow or field... exactly as it was at the beginning of this journey... and all around you is spacious and clear...

Now leaving this open landscape... Finding your way slowly back... to this room that we are in... Following the sound of my voice... back here to where we have all gathered...

Focusing on the sound of your breath... Feeling your feet grounding you to Mother Earth... Sensing your legs... your back resting against the chair you are in... You may want to stretch your neck... or your arms... or shake out your hands and feet... moving your body in some way that feels deliciously good to you in this moment...

And when you are ready... opening your eyes... taking your time... I will wait for you... Remembering that all is well...

Council Circle

Take a few conscious breaths… and allow your eyes to close… or keep a soft downward gaze if that feels right… Giving your body permission to relax… and to be comfortable…

Allowing your body to experience the contact that it makes with the chair and with the floor… and adjusting any parts of you… shifting however you need to… in order to be just a bit more comfortable… resting here now…

As you tune in to the rhythm of your breathing, imagine that when you inhale… you're inhaling a little bit of the sky… and it's very clear and very refreshing… And as you exhale, imagine that you're letting go of whatever you don't need right now… Inhaling the light, clear sky… Exhaling that which does not serve you right now…

Letting the rhythm of your breath be just what it is… a simple and beautiful process of taking in what's fresh and clear… and letting go of what's no longer needed… Each breath you take relaxes and refreshes you… Your breathing and your mind are becoming clearer and clearer… Your body is relaxing a little bit more with each inhale and exhale…

Allowing your imagination to be as open and receptive as you like… Breathing in… and breathing out… I'm inviting you now to take a short inner journey… a magical journey to your inner safe landscape where all kinds of special things are always happening…

Continuing to breath in… and out… in… and out… I invite you to use your imagination now to bring yourself to a very safe place… where you will meet with three chosen Council members… But first… if you like… go ahead and take some time to explore this beautiful place before we invite them in… The four of you will be sitting in a circle soon… so find a comfortable place outside in nature… or inside somewhere special… or wherever it is that you feel comfortable having this meeting…

So now you are exploring this space… and making it ready for these archetypal Council energies who will be joining you today to offer wisdom… taking in your environment… noticing what you see… hear… smell… feel… And also… paying attention to what you need to do to make this space ready for your circle meeting… Taking your time… Enjoying this sacred place you are creating…

And now… when you are ready… if you choose to… go ahead and invite your three chosen Council members into this sacred circle that you have created and prepared… Calling each one by name… watching as they arrive… greeting them… allowing yourself to be greeted by them… Perhaps noticing how each one is different… yet noticing also how each one holds the same intention of love and guidance… specifically for you…

After the four of you are seated, take a look around… sensing the love and wisdom that is flowing from your Council guides to you… and back again… Listening also to what is happening inside of you… Is there something going on in your life right now that you would like some help with?… Is there an issue… or a person… or a situation in your life… that you are struggling with…that you need some help with?… If so… go ahead and tell these kind, loving Council members exactly what you are dealing with… Ask any questions that you like… and then just listen… simply listen to each one in turn… What are they saying to you?… Or maybe they are showing you something… What is their response?… Just allowing whatever comes forth from them… to come forth…

Taking another minute now in conversation with your Council guides…

And now… finding a way to thank each of them for joining you today… feeling their love and wisdom blessing you…

It's time to start thinking about coming back from this inner journey now… but first… say good-bye to your Council members… knowing as you say good-bye… that you can come back to this sacred circle with them any time you wish… just by closing your eyes and imagining yourself here…

Then… when you are ready… slowly and mindfully leave the circle… finding your way back the same way you came in… walking slowly… stepping easily… becoming mindful of your breath…

Now coming back to the room that we are in… feeling your feet grounding you to the earth… sensing all the many parts of your body… feeling your chest rising and falling with each breath… maybe stretching in some way that makes your body feel good…

Choosing to open your eyes when you are ready… Please take your time… I will wait for you… All is well.

Butterfly Woman 1

Taking a deep breath now… allowing your eyes to close when you are ready… or keeping a soft downward gaze… Giving your body whatever permission it needs to more fully relax… shifting any part of you that needs to make itself a bit more comfortable… and maybe even a bit more comfortable than that… Ahhh… Very good…

And as you tune in to the rhythm of your breath, imagine that when you inhale… you're inhaling a little bit of the sky… and it's very clear and refreshing… As you exhale… imagine that you're letting go of everything that's no longer needed…

Inhaling the refreshing, clear sky… Exhaling anything that you no longer need… Inhaling… Exhaling… Inhaling… Exhaling…

Allowing your imagination to be as open and receptive as it wants to be for now… Breathing in… and breathing out… I'm going to invite you now… to take a magical journey to your inner world where all kinds of special things are happening… You can choose to take this inner journey… or you can choose to stay right where you are in this quiet space of breathing in… and out…

If you are choosing to come on this inner journey… I invite you to imagine that you are walking in a beautiful space outdoors… somewhere in nature that you really love… a special place where you feel safe… where you feel more like yourself… This might be a place you have visited in the past… or it might be a place that exists only in your imagination… Taking yourself there now… walking slowly around… exploring this space… Do you hear any sounds?… Are there certain scents that belong to this place?… What do you see?… What can you touch?…

As you are walking… exploring… you notice up ahead that there is a woman wearing a long gown or dress… She is standing very still… and her back is to you… You are feeling curious… so you continue walking towards her… What color is the garment she is wearing?… What color is her hair?… Is she wearing anything else that you can see from here?… As you move closer… you notice that she is standing with her arms lifted up… and there are beautiful butterflies fluttering all around her… A few of them are in her hair and several are on her gown… In fact… the air surrounding her is sprinkled with a rainbow of butterflies…

Now she is greeting you by name… but she is still facing away from you… and you are listening to her say your name… and you are feeling her call of welcome in every cell of your body…

When you ask why she doesn't turn around… she tells you that she is facing forward because she wants to remind you that it's time to stop looking back at how things were… and it's time to stand tall in the light and look ahead… to how things are going to be… She tells you that she is called Butterfly Woman… that she is an agent of change for you… if you want her to be…

Now she is inviting you to walk closer… to stand right beside her… amidst the quiet hush of butterfly wings…

You can choose to do this if you want… or you can stay right where you are…
It's up to you… It's your choice to make… So… now… standing beside her…
or staying where you are… go ahead and continue this conversation with Butterfly Woman on your own for a few minutes… Ask her anything you want to ask her… about what you might be leaving behind… or about what you might be moving towards… Or you might be asking her about how she can be an agent of change for you…

Simply listen… or watch her response…
Perhaps the butterflies are responding to your question as well…

It's almost time to come back from this inner journey for now… but first… I invite you to find a way to say farewell for now to Butterfly Woman… knowing in your heart that she is always here within you… ready to guide you through any transition that you need to make… any change that you might choose to make… Knowing also that she is always ready to hold your hand through the changes and transformations that you are beginning to make in your life…

And now bringing yourself back to this room that we are in… taking a few moments to focus on your breath once again… feeling your feet on the floor grounding you… sensing your legs and your back as they touch the surface of your chair… feeling your chest rising and falling with each breath… moving your body gently in any way that feels just right for you in this moment…

Then in your own time… gently open your eyes… There is no rush…
Take your time… I will wait for you… All is well…

Butterfly Woman 2

Taking a deep breath now… allowing your eyes to close when you are ready… or keeping a soft downward gaze… Giving your body whatever permission it needs to more fully relax… shifting any part of you that needs to make itself a bit more comfortable… and maybe even a bit more comfortable than that… Ahhh… Very good…

And as you tune in to the rhythm of your breath, imagine that when you inhale… you're inhaling a little bit of the sky… and it's very clear and refreshing… As you exhale… imagine that you're letting go of everything that's no longer needed…

Inhaling the refreshing, clear sky… Exhaling anything that you no longer need… Inhaling… Exhaling… Inhaling… Exhaling…

Allowing your imagination to be as open and receptive as it wants to be for now… breathing in… and breathing out… I invite you now to imagine that you are back in your special place outdoors… Imagine yourself walking around… exploring… if you like… grounding yourself in the beauty of nature that is present all around you… the sights… the sounds… the smells…

And as you are exploring… make your way back to Butterfly Woman… If you choose to… walk right up to her and stand beside her… standing there with her in the midst of the many beautiful butterflies that seem to be everywhere…

Spend a few moments now… talking with Butterfly Woman about the particular transition you are going through in your life…

And watch as Butterfly Woman claps her hands lightly three times… The butterflies who have been flying around in front of her rise up… and up… Now you are seeing that there is a door several feet in front of you… Notice what kind of a door it is… Is it open… or closed… or somewhere in between?… What is this door made of?… What color is it?… How big is it?…

Butterfly Woman is offering you her hand now… She is inviting you to walk towards the door with her… You can choose to do this… or you can choose to stay where you are for now… It's up to you… The door will stay there for you as long as you need… until you are sure that you are ready…

If you are ready now… go ahead and walk with Butterfly Woman to this door. .. Notice if you are walking on your own… or if she is carrying you… or if you are walking side by side holding hands with her…

When you come to the door… if you choose to… only if you choose to… take a step through… just one step… and take a look around you… What is on the other side of the door?... Allow the butterflies to come with you if you would like them with you…

You can stay close to the door if you want to… or you can walk a little farther away from the door and explore for a few minutes… Becoming more aware of your feelings as you walk through the door… and honoring these feelings as precious compass points on your beautiful journey… Allowing your feelings and your inner knowing to guide you forward on this next part of your life journey…

As you're exploring this new place in your life… you notice a treasure chest of some sort… and you are moving towards it… What does this chest look like?... How does it feel when you touch it?... Now you can decide to open the treasure chest… or not… It's up to you… If you want to open it… go ahead and open it now… and inside you find a special gift waiting for you… It is a gift from the other side of the door… What gift is waiting for you here?...

It's almost time to leave now… so pick up your gift and carry it with you…
Moving back through the door now… finding a way to say good-bye to Butterfly Woman… knowing that she is always here for you… waiting… smiling… among the butterflies… your own personal agent of change… guiding you through transition…

And now bringing yourself back to this room that we are in… Taking a few moments to focus on your breath once again… Feeling your feet on the floor grounding you… Sensing your legs and your back as they touch the surface of your chair… Feeling your chest rising and falling with each breath… Moving your body gently in any way that feels just right for you in this moment…

Then in your own time… gently open your eyes… There is no rush…
Take your time… I will wait for you… All is well…

Part 6

Animal Companions

*It is... through the world of the imagination
which takes us beyond the restrictions of provable fact,
that we touch the hem of truth.*

~ Madeleine L'Engle

Meeting an Animal Guide

Visualize at your feet a soft blanket or sheet… You can make it any color that you choose… Whatever color it is… it is giving you a sense of well-being… of feeling loved… And just imagine now that you are pulling this blanket or sheet slowly up and over your body… Feel it moving over your feet… relaxing them… Feel it moving over your legs… relaxing them… Imagine the blanket moving over your stomach… removing all tension… and over your back… removing all stress…

With each breath… you are becoming a little bit more relaxed… more and more peaceful… breathing in… breathing out… Now continue to pull the blanket over your chest and arms… relaxing them… relaxing them… And as you move this soft blanket or sheet over your neck… the muscles of your neck relax… and the blanket shapes itself into a hood that covers the back of your head lightly… And you can sense your face muscles relaxing too… Now you are completely enveloped in this soft sheet or blanket… and you feel its color soaking into your body and soul… as you continue to relax a bit more… and a bit more with each breath…

I invite you now to see yourself walking down a path that is outside somewhere in nature… Choose your favorite place in nature… and walk there slowly now… Looking around you… noticing everything… shapes… colors… growing things… things of nature… And noticing also any sounds in your environment… any smells… any feelings…

And in your imagination… you are coming to a clearing… a spacious clearing is in front of you on your path now… I invite you to walk to the very center of this clearing and twirl around for a moment… Fling your arms out wide… and spin lightly in the center if you like… Moving in some way that delights you… whatever that means for you in this moment…

Coming to stillness now… slowly… slowly… You are standing very still… in the center of this clearing… You are standing completely still now…

And if it feels right to you… imagine that every animal known to humankind is slowly entering this safe wide space that you are standing in… They are forming a big circle all around you… Imagine the animals coming in one by one… listening to the sounds they make… This is a very safe place for you and for them… Just watching and listening… as they form a large circle all around you…

You are feeling very curious about these animals… You believe they each have wisdom to share… and you are certain that one of these animals has something very special to give you right now at this moment… So turn slowly… slowly around… in the center of the circle… and say out loud in your imagination… "Who wants to come forward now?"… and then watch… just watch what happens…

Perhaps an animal has joined you in the center of the circle… Whatever animal it is, welcome it with a smile and curious delight… Be as open as you can to its energy… Ask it who it is… and what wisdom it wants to share with you today… You may choose to just listen to him or her… or you might choose to have a conversation…

If an animal has not come forward… know that this is perfectly okay… know that you can return here to this circle in your imagination at any time… and for now… just bask in all of this animal energy that is present for you today…

It's almost time to leave the circle now… but before you go… if an animal has come forward… you might choose to ask this animal to touch a part of your body… and simply watch what it does when you ask this… Now ask your animal guide if it has a gift that it wants to give you before you leave… a gift to take with you so that you can remember this special encounter always… and then watch what happens… What gift does your animal give you?…

Now… find a special way to thank your animal friend… And then perhaps bow t o all of the animals that surround you… or simply wave good-bye to them…

Then in your own time… and in your own way… step out of the circle… and follow your safe path back… and back… .until you are able to feel your body resting on your chair…

Bringing yourself back to your breath… and back to your body once again… You might want to lightly flex your fingers and toes… or gently shake out your arms and legs… moving your body in some way that brings you back to our gathering… You may want to shake off the beautiful blanket or sheet that you've been wearing… Or you may decide to leave it on…

Opening your eyes when you feel ready… Taking your time… I will wait for you… Remembering that all is well…

Sacred Animals Circle

Begin by making your body as comfortable as you can… Closing your eyes when you are ready… or choosing to keep your eyes open with a soft downward gaze… Focusing on your breath… as the air comes in… and as it goes out… in… and out… Feeling your chest rising and falling… rising and falling…

Giving the weight of your body over to the support of your chair… leaning back… surrendering… Giving the weight of your thoughts and feelings over to the presence of the Divine… however you imagine the Divine to be present in your life today…

Now you are even more relaxed… and in your imagination I invite you to imagine a path… It can be any kind of a path… a little trail in the woods… or a country road… or a brick walkway in a garden… This path can be anywhere you want it to be… by the ocean… in the city… up a mountain… in a meadow…

Wherever this path is… know that it was created just for you… Know too that it is a safe and friendly path… and as you start walking on this path… you are noticing a lovely sense of delight and anticipation…

Following this path… trusting that it will lead you wherever you need to go…

Looking around you as you walk… and just noticing… sights… colors… sounds… smells… textures…

As you continue on this path… you will soon be finding a Sacred Circle… This is a very special place where your Animal Companions will gather once you invite them in to the Circle…

Continuing to walk now… and pausing whenever you want to simply enjoy your surroundings…

Now… up ahead you can see the space where your Sacred Circle awaits you… So go ahead and make your way over to this sacred space now…

As you approach your Sacred Circle… you notice that there is a beautiful cloth or rug laid down in the center of it… If you like… go to that beautiful cloth or rug… and stand in the middle of it… reveling in the beauty, the sweetness… of this space…

Know that some of your Animal Companions are going to join you very soon… and remember… you don't have to do anything for them to join you… Remember also that your Animal Companions have already chosen you… You don't need to decide… They have been waiting for the opportunity to introduce themselves to you… They have been waiting... for a moment just like this one... so simply hold love and acceptance and openness in your heart... and they will reveal themselves to you... all in good time...

We're going to start by focusing on the first chakra... the root chakra...This is the area at the base of your spine... Begin by breathing into this area of your body... If you find that difficult, it's okay....Just concentrate on or think about that part of your body... This energy center is often associated with the ideas of safety... survival... home... healthy relationship to the earth... This chakra is all about your right to have... and your right as a human being to be here...

As you focus on the energy that is in your first chakra... at the base of your spine... imagine yourself squatting down in the center of your Sacred Circle... Then say or sing or just think these words into the wilderness around you... I invite my first chakra animal to come forward now...

And then watch what happens... Who comes forward into the Circle with you?... You may just sit in silence with this animal... or you may play a game with it... or have a conversation... or you may simply sit and wait... Perhaps this animal is not ready to come forward yet... Remember, whatever happens is perfectly okay...

If you've been conversing or playing with an animal here in this chakra... thank them for spending time with you... and then ask them to step back into their place in the Circle while you continue on this journey...

Now.... Take some time to focus on your second chakra... This is the sacral chakra... and it is located in the curve of the sacrum, where your pelvis is... Begin by breathing into this area of your body... or just focus on that part of your body now.... This energy center is often associated with creativity... emotions... and sexuality... This chakra is all about your right to feel... and your right as a human being to want... to desire...

As you focus on the energy that is in your second chakra energy center... Imagine yourself standing with your legs spread apart but completely balanced... Then say or sing or just think these words into the wilderness around you... I invite my second chakra animal to come forward now...

And then watch what happens... Who comes forward into the Circle with you?... You may just sit in silence with this animal... or you may play a game with it... or have a conversation... or you may simply sit and wait... Perhaps this animal is not ready to come forward yet... Remember, whatever happens is perfectly okay...

If you've been conversing or playing with an animal... thank them for spending time with you… and then ask them to step back into their place in the circle while you continue on this journey…

Now let's spend some time in your third chakra… This is the area of your solar plexus… just above your belly button and below your breastbone… Begin by breathing into this area of your body… or focusing on it… This energy center is your personal power center… and is often associated with the ideas of effective action… authenticity… and personal power… This chakra is all about your right to act… the right to own your own personal power…

As you focus on the energy that is in your third chakra… above your stomach… imagine yourself standing straight and tall with your arms outstretched… in the center of your Sacred Circle… Then say or sing or just think these words into the wilderness around you… I invite my third chakra animal to come forward now…

And then watch what happens… Who comes forward into the Circle with you?… You may just sit in silence with this animal… or you may play a game with it… or have a conversation… or you may simply sit and wait… Perhaps this animal is not ready to come forward yet… Remember, whatever happens is perfectly okay…

If you've been conversing or playing with an animal… thank them for spending time with you… and then ask them to step back into their place in the circle while you continue on this journey…

Now… Take some time to focus on your fourth chakra… This is your heart chakra and it is located in the center of your chest… Begin by breathing into this area of your body… or just focusing on it… Your fourth chakra… This energy center is often associated with the ideas of love of self… love of others… community… and relationships… This chakra is all about your right to love… and your right to be loved…

As you focus on the energy that is in your fourth chakra energy center… imagine yourself standing in the center of your Sacred Circle… with your hands resting lightly over the center of your chest… Then say or sing or just think these words into the wilderness around you… I invite my fourth chakra animal to come forward now…

And then watch what happens… Who comes forward into the Circle with you?… You may just sit in silence with this animal… or you may play a game with it… or have a conversation… or you may simply sit and wait… Perhaps this animal is not ready to come forward yet… Remember, whatever happens is perfectly okay…

If you've been conversing or playing with an animal… thank them for spending time with you… and then ask them to step back into their place in the circle while you continue on this journey…

Now… Let's focus on the fifth chakra… This is your throat chakra… located in the lower part of your neck… Begin by breathing into this area of your body… or just focusing your attention there now… Your fifth chakra… This energy center is often associated with the ideas of communication and self-expression… This chakra is all about your right to speak the truth… and to hear the truth…

As you focus on the energy that is in your fifth chakra…in your throat… imagine yourself slowly and gently rolling your neck from side to side… Then say or sing these words into the wilderness around you… I invite my fifth chakra animal to come forward now…

And then watch what happens… Who comes forward into the Circle with you?… You may just sit in silence with this animal… or you may play a game with it… or have a conversation… or you may simply sit and wait… Perhaps this animal is not ready to come forward yet… Remember, whatever happens is perfectly okay…

If you've been conversing or playing with an animal… thank them for spending time with you… and then ask them to step back into their place in the circle while you continue on this journey…

Let's focus on your sixth chakra now… This is the third eye chakra and it is located in the center of your forehead, between your eyebrows… Begin by breathing into this area of your body… or just focusing your attention there now… Your sixth chakra… This energy center is often associated with the ideas of intuition… imagination… and intellect… and of being able to see with your inner eye as well as your outer eyes… This chakra is all about your right to see… both inwardly and outwardly…

As you focus on the energy that is in your sixth chakra energy center… in the center of your forehead… imagine yourself standing in the center of your Sacred Circle with your eyes lightly closed… Then say or sing or just think these words into the wilderness around you… I invite my sixth chakra animal to come forward now…

And then watch what happens… Who comes forward into the Circle with you?… You may just sit in silence with this animal… or you may play a game with it… or have a conversation… or you may simply sit and wait… Perhaps this animal is not ready to come forward yet… Remember, whatever happens is perfectly okay…

If you've been conversing or playing with an animal… thank them for spending time with you… and then ask them to step back into their place in the circle while you continue on this journey…

It's time now to focus on the seventh chakra… This is your crown chakra… and it is located just above the top of your head… Begin by breathing into this area of your body… or just focusing your attention there… Your seventh chakra… This energy center is often associated with the ideas of self-awareness… and spiritual connection… This chakra is all about your right to know… and your right to a spiritual connection to the Divine…

As you focus on the energy that is in your seventh chakra… just above your head… imagine yourself standing with your arms lifted high into the air… reaching toward the heavens… Then say or sing these words into the wilderness around you… I invite my seventh chakra animal to come forward now…

And then watch what happens… Who comes forward into the Circle with you?… You may just sit in silence with this animal… or you may play a game with it… or have a conversation… or you may simply sit and wait… Perhaps this animal is not ready to come forward yet… Remember… whatever happens is perfectly okay….

If you've been conversing or playing with an animal… thank them for spending time with you… and then ask them to step back into their place in the circle while you continue on this journey…

Now, your time in your Sacred Animals Circle is almost done for now… but before you leave… go ahead and slowly turn around… perhaps bowing to each of the animals who have joined your circle today… There may be seven animals in your Circle… or just a few… or only one… It doesn't matter… It's all okay… Simply bow to any animals that are there… making eye contact with each one as you do… one at a time…

If no animals have shown up today… that is okay too… Know that you are creating this special place just for them… and when they feel it is time… they will come to you if you continue to show up for them…

Still standing in the center of your Sacred Circle now… just imagine that each animal there is shining its beautiful precious light onto you… in the center… all at once…

and you are just savoring the feeling of love and light that washes over you as they do this… If no animals are here yet… simply imagine Divine Love shining down on you from above… and filling you with a feeling of safety… and of being loved…

It's time to start thinking about leaving your Sacred Circle now… but first say good-bye to your animals… and let them know that you will be back soon…

And when you are ready… slowly and mindfully leave the circle… Find your way back the same way you came in…. Walk as slowly as you need to…

Becoming aware now of your breath moving in and out of your nose… Coming back to this room… Feeling your feet on the floor… Now feeling your legs and your back against the chair … Coming back to your body now… Maybe stretching your body in a way that feels really good to you in this moment… Feeling your chest rising and falling with each breath…

And when you are ready… only when you are ready… go ahead and open your eyes… Please take your time… I will wait for you… All is well…

Part 7

Spirituality

The power of imagination makes us infinite.

~ John Muir

Circled on a Map

> This place where you are right now
> God circled on a map for you
> Wherever your eyes and arms and heart can move
> against the earth and the sky,
> the beloved has bowed there-
> the beloved has bowed there knowing
> you were coming…
>
> ~ Hafiz

When you are ready, allow yourself to come to stillness… Give yourself permission to come home to yourself for these next several minutes… Give yourself permission to come home to Spirit… to the One that holds the many parts of your world… Paying attention to your breath… not trying to change it… Just noticing as you breathe in… and noticing as you breathe out… Breathing in the stillness that is always inside of you… breathing out any inner chaos… Breathing in peace…. breathing out any inner conflicts that have been going on… Giving yourself permission to just breathe in… to just breathe out… and to simply relax…

And as you come into this beautiful sense of centering… of coming home to yourself… imagine that you are sitting in an ancient room full of maps and charts… Take a moment to walk around the room… and as you do… notice that everything in this room is related to your own personal journey through life… Acquaint yourself with the many atlases and diagrams… navigational tools… drawings of sacred places… all of them representing your life… Lands that are known and unknown to you are represented on all of these maps… and charts… books… and tools… Take a moment now to explore this place… this navigational homage to your own journey…

In a moment, you see a Wise One standing in the doorway… and now you have the choice to invite this Wise One in… or you can choose to say "not now"… and to continue to explore on your own… If you choose to let the Wise One in… see that he or she is gesturing for you to sit down at a big table in the center of the room… If it feels right… go ahead and sit down… and now watch as your Wise One goes to one of the shelves… takes out an ancient volume… brings it to you at the table… and opens it to a specific page… Just watching for a moment… You notice that there is a beautiful map on this page... It is exquisitely etched on silk-like paper... If you like... take a moment to run your hands over the map... Feel how beautiful it is to touch...

Now your Wise One points to a specific place on this map... It is circled in a glowing golden light... Listen as your Wise One speaks... "This is where you are right now on your life's journey"... he or she says gently... "God circled this place... on this map... for you"...

Give yourself a moment to absorb these words.... This place where you are right now... God circled on this map for you... Notice how you feel when you hear these words... Pay attention to the "place" that is circled on the map before you... Where is it?... Is it somewhere you planned to go?... Have you been in this place a long time... or a short time?... Is it somewhere you'd rather not be... or is it somewhere you don't want to leave?...

Whatever the answer... take a moment now to absorb the sacred knowledge that you are exactly where you are supposed to be... You are exactly where you need to be... and remember that this place where you are right now is either a destination... or another stepping stone on your journey... and that you and you alone can choose which it is...

Take a moment now to thank your Wise One for showing you the map... and the circle on the map... If you choose... ask for a gift or a symbol to take back with you to remind you of this inner journey today...

And when you are ready... take another moment to come back to your breath... Notice the air as it comes into your body and fills your lungs... Then notice how it feels to release the breath through your nose or mouth... Follow the sound of my voice back to this present moment... back... and back... to our gathering today...

If it feels good to do so... you might want to stretch your fingers and toes... move your head and neck slowly from side to side... And in whatever way feels good to you... offer a prayer of thanksgiving for wherever you are on your journey at this time... remembering the comforting words of Hafiz... This place where you are right now... God circled on a map for you...

Opening your eyes when you feel ready... Taking your time... I will wait for you... and remember that all is well.

Plugging Into Source

Begin by bringing your body into a comfortable position… keeping your spine straight… adjusting any part of your body… doing whatever you need to do to adjust your body so that it is feeling ahhhh… just right… so comfortable… Coming to a gradual stillness… coming to that place where you can hear your breath… and just listen to your breath for a moment… not trying to change it… just listening to it… Rising… falling… Breath coming in…. breath going out… You have nowhere to go and nothing to do right now… Just relaxing your body… becoming calmer and more peaceful… as you bring your awareness to your breath…

Breathing just a bit more slowly now… and setting the intention that during this quiet time you will be plugging into Source… or whatever you choose to call Source… God… Spirit… The One… All That Is… Just setting that intention now… feeling that longing to connect to Source… to rest in the presence of Spirit for a while…

And now imagine that you are standing up… right in this room that you are in… just imagine standing up for a moment… still feeling that longing to plug into Source… that desire to fill yourself with Source Energy….

Looking down now… you see that your feet and legs are attached to many different cords and the cords are all plugged into outlets all around the room… You realize that you can't move… that you are tethered to these cords… You realize that you can't really plug into Source.. until you unplug yourself from all of these outlets that are depleting your energy…

Each of these cords represents some aspect of your own life… a project… a class… a person… a task… a situation… a pattern or way of being that you have outgrown… a challenge that you are facing…

So now… if you choose to do so… take some time and name each cord that is holding you here… Name it gently and without judgement… and then unplug it from the wall… slowly… taking your time…

Reminding yourself that you aren't unplugging from these things forever… just for now… so you can have more space to plug into Source….

Unplugging the cords… one by one… the cords that keep you tethered and bound… unable to truly connect with Source…

And now… when you are ready… when most of the cords are unplugged… stand right where you are in your imagination… and stretch… moving your legs and arms in a sweet dance of freedom… enjoying, savoring this spaciousness you've given yourself for a little while…

If a thought comes up… just find the cord and the outlet… and unplug it… You don't need that thought right now… Just let it go….

When you are ready… imagine that you are coming again to stillness… and you are opening up the space at the top of your head… A beautiful white light is reaching down towards you… This is the light of Source… and the wider the opening at the top of your body… the more light can pour into you… soothing your mind… calming your body… energizing your spirit….

Take some time now to connect with Source in this way… opening… opening… allowing the light to fill you… bathe you… love you…

If a distracting or critical thought seeps into your mind… give yourself permission to know that it's just a thought… It has no power… It is not who you are… and simply unplug yourself from it…

Feeling the power of Source seeping into your breath… your heart… and your life… feeling this light radiating through your body… and out into the world…

Any thought that enters your mind… remember that you can simply disconnect from it… by naming it and unplugging its cord…

Remembering also now that Source doesn't communicate with words… but with breath… with light… with energy… and allowing yourself to bask in this Source energy a while longer…

It's nearing time to end this journey… so begin to come back by expressing gratitude to Source for this time of connection… If you can… find a way to thank Source without words…

And then you might want to close the space over your head just a little bit… until it feels just right for your return… Not shutting off the light of Source completely… just letting there be enough light there… in your head and in your heart… to sustain you in your daily work in the world…

At this time… you might also want to re-plug yourself back into only those projects… or people… or tasks… that you need to focus on for the rest of your day… Naming each cord as you plug it into its outlet… Noting how it serves you in your world… And when you are connected back to your life… begin once again to become aware again of your breathing… Your chest is rising and falling with each breath… Allowing the sound of my voice to bring you back to our gathering… stretching and breathing more deeply…

Opening your eyes when you are ready… Taking your time… I will wait for you… Remembering that all is well…

Journey to the Center of You

Take a moment now to make yourself as comfortable as you can… consciously relaxing any part of your body that feels tense or tight… giving yourself this time to be still… to journey within… to your center…

Paying attention to your breath for a moment… not trying to change it… just being with your breathing… in… and out… in … and out… Noticing how the air feels coming in… and how it feels going out… Breathing… Relaxing… Breathing… Relaxing… There's nowhere to go… and there's nothing to do but simply be here with yourself… journeying within…

And now in your imagination… I invite you to find yourself in your inner sanctuary… a safe place in your imagination where you can go to escape the pressures and stress of your daily life… It might be a cave… or a sacred forest… a cottage by the sea… a church… an oasis in the stars… Your inner sanctuary is a place where you feel loved… and safe… secure… and grounded… There may be others in this space… others whom you have invited… or you might be alone… Take a moment now to explore this inner sanctuary space… What do you see?… What do you hear?… Smell?… Feel?…

Now I invite you to look around… wherever you are… and start looking for the pathway that leads to your center… That's right… you are going on a journey directly to your center… whatever that means to you… So if it feels right… take a few minutes to look around inside of yourself… until you find the beginning of the path or road that leads to your center… Look carefully… You will know when you find it… It might be a winding path like a labyrinth… or it might be a ladder… or a simple stone walkway… maybe a stream… a spiral… a set of stepping stones… Your path might look like a river of fire… or even a rainbow… Just spend some time now looking around your inner world for the beginning of this sacred pathway… the pathway that leads you to your center…

Once you've found it… I invite you to pause at the beginning of the path and look around… noticing where you are… and what is there… what you see… what you hear… what you can touch or smell…

You have found a safe starting point for your own journey to your center…

And now… if you choose… begin to move slowly forward on this path …
You might be walking… or you might be swimming… or flying… skipping…
or even dancing… Feel free to move in whatever way feels right to you…
and notice… as you begin this journey… if anyone is with you on your path…
Perhaps you are choosing to make this journey to your center alone… or perhaps
you have invited a safe loved one with you… Either way, it's good… It's your journey…
so you get to decide… You may even discover different beings such as animals…
humans… spirit beings… traveling with you… the farther in that you travel…
Simply allow this journey to be whatever it is… knowing that you are safe
and in control at all times…

Continuing to follow this pathway as it leads you to your very center…
Traveling inward… inward… Noticing how it feels to be moving
so confidently towards your center…

And when you have arrived at the center of your being…
just pause for a moment here… Pause… and breathe in this very sacred place
that exists within the center of your self… Pause… Breathe… Notice… Feel…

What is it that you see or sense here?…What images come to you in your center?…
What does your particular spark of the Divine look like here?…

What can you hear?… What can you taste… touch… smell?…
Allowing whatever comes to you to be perfect as it is… for this is your journey…
and this is the center… the heart… the SoulEssence of beautiful, precious you…
Taking this time now to explore your center… exploring… allowing…
noticing… feeling…

It's nearing time to leave your Center now… but before you do… if it feels right…
take a few moments to express gratitude to the Divine for this space inside of you…
for the sacred spark of the Divine that lives within you… for any gifts you have been
given today just by visiting this sacred place… this sacred center of your being…

And then… when you feel ready… begin to follow the path back outwards…
outwards from the center… taking your time… pausing along the way if you need to…
knowing that you carry this Center with you at all times…
knowing that you can consciously return here just by closing your eyes…
and following that same inner path…

Following your special path back outwards now… outwards…
following the path towards the sound of my voice…
bringing yourself back to this day… to our gathering…

Taking your time… moving slowly… stretching gently if you need to…
so you can come back more fully to your body…

Open your eyes only when you feel completely ready…
Please take your time… I will wait for you… All is well…

Part 8

Miscellaneous

Some stories are true that never happened.

~ Elie Wiesel

Yellow Brick Road- Part 1

Take a moment now to shift into a comfortable position… paying attention to any part of your body that might need to stretch or relax a bit more…

Taking three slow breaths consciously now… In… and out… in… and out… in… and out… Ahhh… Closing your eyes if it feels comfortable to do so… or simply keeping a soft downward gaze… Imagining now that every part of your body is comfortable and relaxed… Enjoying this little respite from your busy life…There's nowhere to go… and nothing to do for this next little while… except to relax… and to rest… relaxing just a little bit more… and resting just a little bit more…

In your mind's eye… I invite you to picture yourself in Munchkin Land… but instead of Munchkins, you are seeing all the members of your Community… family, friends, teachers, pets… from the past as well as the present… They are all here to wish you well on your journey… so spend a moment among them now… listening to their well wishes… their encouragement… their love…

And now they are fading away… Wave good-bye if you like… and know that you take a little bit of each one of these loved ones with you on your journey today…

As they leave… you notice that you are standing at the beginning of a long and winding road… It is glowing in the sunlight… and it is made of yellow bricks… Yes, it's the Yellow Brick Road… You look off in the distance… and you can see the Emerald City of Oz waaaaaay over there… This Yellow Brick Road can lead you directly to Oz…

As you are wondering if you'll ever be able to follow this winding road all the way to the Emerald City… someone appears before you in a magical swirl of glittery dust… Look… it's your very own Glinda… What does your Glinda look like?... What is she wearing?... Find a way to greet your Glinda… and then listen as she asks you what it is that you hope to find when you get to Oz… "What is it that you really want right now in your life?"…and then take a moment to let an answer rise up from your heart… When you are ready… say to Glinda…
"What I really, really want right now, more than anything is…"

Listen now as your version of Glinda affirms you… and reassures you that you can have whatever it is that you really want… that it will be waiting for you when you arrive in Oz… Taking in her words… absorbing her assurance… her confidence… How does it feel to know… to truly believe… that you can have your heart's desire?…

Now Glinda is urging you to begin your journey… and she sprinkles some magic sparkly dust over you… Notice what scent this magical dust carries with it… and notice the colors… Glinda is telling you that the magic dust is to bless you with an open mind… an open heart… and a lot of courage… Imagining now… your mind opening… your heart opening… and a feeling of strength and courage flowing through you…

If it feels right… you can choose to take some steps along the Yellow Brick Road now… or you can stay right here and explore where you are… If you are heading for Oz… and your dreams… go ahead and start walking on the Yellow Brick Road now… leaving Glinda behind as you go… looking around you on the path… feeling safe and secure… heading towards Oz and your dreams…

Continuing to walk… noticing… observing… listening… feeling… As you are walking… you might want to take note of anyone you meet… You might come across the Tin Man… or the Scarecrow… or even the Cowardly Lion… You might meet up with some other fellow journeyers… Just notice who crosses your path as you walk… and listen to any wisdom these fellow travelers might have for you as you follow this Yellow Brick Road to Oz… and your heart's desire…

Remembering as you walk… why you are on this journey to the Emerald City of Oz… Remembering your heart's desire… Maybe even telling your companions what it is that you want the most… and listening also to what they want…

It's almost time to come back now… We will continue this journey later… But for now… make note of where you are on the path… because you'll be coming back to this spot when you return… Saying good-bye to any traveling companions you've encountered… and thanking them for journeying with you today…

And now in your own time… and your own way… traveling back to this room… back… back… following the sound of my voice… slowly and gently…
You might want to stretch any part of your body that's needing to move right now… Grounding yourself back into your breathing body…

When you are ready… gently opening your eyes… Taking your time…
I will wait for you… All is well…

Yellow Brick Road- Part 2

Take a moment now to shift into a comfortable position… paying attention to any part of your body that might need to stretch or relax a bit more…

Taking three slow breaths consciously now… In… and out… in… and out… in… and out… Ahhh… Closing your eyes if it feels comfortable to do so… or simply keeping a soft downward gaze… Imagining now that every part of your body is comfortable and relaxed… Enjoying this little respite from your busy life…There's nowhere to go… and nothing to do for this next little while… except to relax… and to rest… relaxing just a little bit more… and resting just a little bit more…

And now… in your imagination… I invite you to bring yourself back to the place on the Yellow Brick Road where you were the last time you were here… taking in the sights… glancing down at your ruby slippers… or whatever fabulous shoes you are wearing… and noticing how they feel on your feet… wiggling your toes… Thanking these shoes… your inner power… for accompanying you on this journey today… Looking around you now… and paying attention to where you are with all of your senses… What are you seeing… hearing… smelling?… feeling?… If you were traveling with some companions you might choose to call them back to you now… or you can choose to journey in solitude… If you were traveling alone and you'd like a companion or two on this leg of the journey towards Oz… look around and see if someone is there to join you now…

Remembering that you are safe because of Glinda's magical dust… that you are journeying towards your heart's desire with an open heart… an open mind… and much courage… just continue your journey down the Yellow Brick Road… remembering why you are traveling to Oz… remembering your heart's desire… and maybe even saying it out loud in your imagination to yourself or to your companions…

As you are walking you are noticing that you are not on a straight path… There are twists and turns… Maybe there's a stream to cross… or some rocks in your way… Just continuing to navigate the journey with your companions… seen or unseen…

Now you are noticing that you are coming to the edge of a forest… There's no way around it… You'll have to go through it… So… in you go… Noticing how much quieter… and darker it is here… But the Yellow Brick Road is still clearly marked and so you continue to follow it... deeper and deeper into the woods... feeling yourself grounded in your ruby slippers... or whatever fabulous, powerful shoes you are wearing... as you step along the Yellow Brick Road in the woods...

Eventually you come across someone or something that is blocking your path... or maybe more than one being or thing... It might be a Wicked Witch... or maybe it's a sad little Munchkin... It might be a horde of flying monkeys... or someone or something else entirely... Whoever it is... it is trying to stop you from moving towards Oz... towards your heart's desire... So... remembering that you are protected and safe... remembering that this is your journey and that no one can harm you here... I invite you to pay close attention to whoever it is that is intent on stopping you from reaching Oz... stopping you from having what it is that you really want... Who is it?... Is this being alone... or is there more than one?... Just allowing the scene to unfold however it wants to... knowing that you are safe... allowing yourself to be curious...

Paying attention also... to what is being said about your heart's desire... There might be some negativity hurled at you... Nevertheless you are standing still... in your shoes... and listening... knowing that they can't hurt you physically... Just listening to the kinds of things they are telling you... What is it that is getting in the way of your heart's desire?...

Remembering that obstacles come up on any journey... It's perfectly normal... And also knowing that you don't have to believe what your own personal "wicked witch" or "flying monkeys" are telling you about your heart's desire...

So now... you can choose to turn around and go back to the beginning of the Yellow Brick Road... where you began... or you can choose to take a quiet breath and stand firm in your decision to travel onward to Oz... to reach your heart's desire... If you are choosing to move forward... go ahead and use whatever language you need... to get these hindrances out of your way... so you can continue on your journey to Oz... towards whatever it is that you really want...

Noticing that as you tell the hindrances to leave... as you tell them that you choose not to believe them... notice that they diminish in size... and disappear...

Now you are free to continue walking on the Yellow Brick Road... maybe singing with your friends... or maybe just traveling quietly... heading through the forest... and out again into the sunshine... feeling perhaps a bit more powerful than you did when you began… continuing your journey to Oz… to your heart's desire… calm mind… peaceful heart… activated courage…

Walking… walking… journeying on… and now you are approaching Oz… It is brighter and more beautiful than you ever imagined… Your version of Glinda is there to greet you… She smiles and welcomes you with open arms… She leads you into the palace and there you find it… your heart's desire… whatever that is for you right now… If you choose to… go forward and claim it… This is what you've been wanting… what you've been seeking… and now it is yours… How does it feel to have this now?... Take some time to savor the feeling of having it… owning it… making it a permanent part of your life…

It's time to start thinking about coming back… so find a way to thank your version of Glinda… as well as any companions who joined you on your journey… knowing that you are bringing your heart's desire back here with you… that it is truly yours… that you have already claimed it…

You might want to ask for a gift… from Glinda… or from one of your companions… a gift that will help you to remember this journey always…

And now in your own time… and your own way… traveling back to this room… back… back… Following the sound of my voice… slowly and gently returning to our class… You might want to stretch any part of your body that's needing to move right now… Grounding yourself back into your breathing body…

When you are ready… gently open your eyes… Take your time… I will wait for you… All is well…

Gaining Perspective

Allow your body to experience the contact that it makes with the chair and with the floor… and let it adjust itself in any way it needs to in order to be just a little bit more comfortable… Shifting any part of you that needs to move for that settled feeling of ahhh… You can close your eyes when it feels safe and comfortable to do so… or you might choose to keep a soft gaze downwards…

As you tune in to the rhythm of your breath, imagine that when you inhale… you're inhaling a little bit of the sky… and it's very clear and very refreshing… And as you exhale, imagine that you're letting go of whatever you don't need right now… Inhaling the light, clear sky… Exhaling that which does not serve you right now… Letting the rhythm of your breath be just what it is… a simple and beautiful process of taking in what's fresh and clear… and letting go of what's no longer needed…

Each breath you take relaxes and refreshes you… Your breathing and your mind are becoming clearer and clearer… Your body is relaxing a little bit more with each inhale and exhale…

I invite you now… in your imagination… to look into the sky… and begin to think of all the things that can fly… insects… birds… balloons… rockets… airplanes… helicopters… What else comes to mind when you think of things that fly… real things… or imaginary things…

Now… imagine yourself walking out in a large open field… and there… resting there just for you… is your own personal flying machine… Walk all around it now… Notice any colors… its shape… Is there any writing on it?… Any symbols?… Is it making any sounds?… How does it feel if you choose to touch it?…

In a minute, you're going to climb aboard… but before that, I invite you to think of a particular challenge that you're experiencing in your life right now… It might be something to do with your health… or a relationship… Perhaps it's about your job or career… Just choose something in your life that's difficult for you to navigate right now… for whatever reason… Just name it to yourself…

And now listen inside yourself… Maybe there are parts of you that are criticizing you… putting you down about this situation,… this challenge… If so, I invite you to visualize them for a moment… let these inner voices take human form… See them…

Hear them... Thank them for sharing... Know that they are not the only parts of you... and then climb right into the pilot's seat of your flying machine... That's right... You are taking the pilot's seat... and as soon as you are cleared for take-off by your Safety Crew on the ground... you can choose to stay on the ground... or you can taxi your plane slowly... and then a bit faster... until you are gliding right up into the air... flying higher... and a little bit higher... only as high as you choose to fly... and knowing also that your Safety Crew on the ground is keeping you perfectly safe... and that you can choose to land whenever you want to...

Waving good-bye to all those critical... unhelpful... inner voices on the ground... noticing that they are getting smaller and smaller as you continue to fly higher... knowing that you are lifting yourself above some of the old patterns of your life... knowing that you can do this anytime you like... breaking free of the gravity of your old limitations... and just noticing how that feels...

Once you've reached a comfortable altitude... whatever that means for you... go ahead and put your flying machine on autopilot... knowing that you are completely safe... and that your Safety Crew on the ground will notify you if anything needs your attention...

Take a moment now to look below... and think again of the challenging relationship or situation that you named before you got into your flying machine... Notice that from this higher vantage point... you have a much better... clearer perspective on this challenge...

Looking down and behind... you can see where and how that particular challenge began... and you might even be able to notice that you've already made some progress with this challenge in your life...

Looking down directly below... you can see more clearly what is really happening right now in this challenge...

And looking farther ahead... Is it possible that you can see that progress has already been made... or that your next steps are more clear?...

I invite you now to settle back into your pilot's seat... and I'm going to give you two minutes to have a gentle conversation with yourself about this challenging situation or relationship... In this time, I invite you to say only compassionate things to yourself... the kind of conversation you might have with a beloved child who is struggling with something… This talking with yourself is about being kind to yourself about this situation… It's about retaining a sense of humor and balance… about accepting yourself and your situation exactly as it is… You might even want to give yourself some tender encouragement about whatever your next steps are to be…

Taking one more minute… saying loving, gentle, encouraging things to yourself…

Very good… Now… when you are ready… I invite you to look down once again… from this higher perspective… look down once again on the challenge that you've been thinking about… and find a way to bless it… again, from this higher perspective… You might use your hands… or your voice… or your breath… blessing this challenge that you are facing…

Now it's time to start thinking about landing your flying machine… so… back in your pilot's seat… facing forward again… taking your flying machine off of autopilot… flying back… and back… back to where this inner journey began… taking your time… Seeking your safe place to land… down below… and when you find that safe place to land… bringing your flying machine slowly… slowly… back down… If any of it is unclear… know that your Safety Crew on the ground will gladly and smoothly guide you back down… And now… in your own time… landing your amazing flying machine… smoothly… easily…

Very good… Getting out of your flying machine for now… Finding a way to express gratitude to it for the gift of perspective that it gave you today… Knowing that you can take a Perspective Flight any time you like… simply by closing your eyes and taking a breath…

Finding a gentle way now to bring yourself back… into your physical body… Feeling your feet on the floor… noticing the position your legs are in… feeling your back against the chair… Maybe slowly moving your head from side to side… shaking out your hands… or wiggling your feet and legs… Following the sound of my voice back to this room… this gathering…

And when you are ready… gently opening your eyes… There is no rush…
I will wait for you… Take your time… Remembering that all is well…

Enjoying the Ride

Allow your body to experience the contact that it makes with the chair and with the floor… and let it adjust itself in any way it needs to in order to be just a little bit more comfortable… Shifting any part of you that needs to move for that settled feeling of ahhh… You can close your eyes when it feels safe and comfortable to do so… or you might choose to keep a soft gaze downwards…

As you tune in to the rhythm of your breath, imagine that when you inhale… you're inhaling a little bit of the sky… and it's very clear and very refreshing… And as you exhale, imagine that you're letting go of whatever you don't need right now… Inhaling the light, clear sky… Exhaling that which does not serve you right now… Letting the rhythm of your breath be just what it is… a simple and beautiful process of taking in what's fresh and clear… and letting go of what's no longer needed…

Each breath you take relaxes and refreshes you… Your breathing and your mind are becoming clearer and clearer… Your body is relaxing a little bit more with each inhale and exhale…

Very good… Now… activating your imagination… I invite you to look up into the sky… and begin to think of all the things that can fly… Insects… birds… balloons… rockets… airplanes… helicopters… What else comes to mind when you think of things that fly…

Now… imagine yourself walking out in a large open field… and there… sitting there just for you… is your own personal flying machine… Walk all around it now… Notice any colors… its shape… Is there any writing on it?… Any symbols?… Is it making any sounds?… How does it feel when you touch it?… Are there any good smells in the air around you?…

If you choose to… go ahead and climb right on board… and then make your way into the pilot's seat of your flying machine… That's right… You are taking the pilot's seat… and as soon as you are cleared for take-off by your Safety Crew on the ground… you can choose to stay on the ground… or you can taxi your plane slowly… and then a bit faster… until you are gliding right up into the air… flying higher… and a little bit higher… only as high as you choose to fly… and knowing also that your Safety Crew on the ground is keeping you safe… and that you can choose to land whenever you want to…

As you continue to pilot your own plane… take a look around you… it's a perfect day for flying… the skies are clear… and you can see for miles… Take a moment to feel the thrill of this flight… Remembering how safe you are… and how your Safety Crew is looking out for you at all times…

Now… I invite you to take a "beauty flight" just for the fun of it… If you choose to… fly yourself to a place that fills you with beauty and awe… There is no reason to go here except that you want to… and that you enjoy it… It might be somewhere you've already been… or it might be an imaginary place… Fly yourself there now… Allow yourself to be lifted… by joy… delight… wonder… and magic…

If you choose to… you can bring your flying machine lower… so you can really see and savor this beautiful place… If you find a safe place to land… you can do so if you'd like to explore on foot… Take two minutes for this beauty flight now…

Taking one more minute… Noticing the pleasure that you feel… in your body… in your mind… your spirit… just being here in this place you've chosen just for the enjoyment of it…

Very good… It's almost time to start thinking about coming back now… If you landed your flying machine… please find your way back to it… Climb back into the pilot's seat… Soar your way back into the sky… remembering again how safe you are…

Flying back… and back… back to where this inner journey began… taking your time… seeking your safe place to land… down below… And when you find that safe place to land… bringing your flying machine slowly… slowly… back down… If any of it is unclear… know that your Safety Crew on the ground will guide you back down… And now… in your own time… landing your amazing flying machine… smoothly… easily…

Very good… Getting out of your flying machine for now… Finding a way to express gratitude to it for this gift of pleasure and enjoyment that it gave you today… Knowing that you can enjoy a flight like this any time you like… simply by closing your eyes and taking a breath…

Finding a gentle way now to bring yourself back into your physical body… Feeling your feet on the floor, noticing the position your legs are in, feeling your back against the chair… Maybe slowly moving your head from side to side… shaking out your hands… or wiggling your feet and legs… Following the sound of my voice back to this room, this place, this time…

And when you are ready… gently opening your eyes… There is no rush… I will wait for you… Take your time… Remembering that all is well…

Gratitudes

*We must find time to stop
and thank the people who
make a difference in our lives.*

~ John F. Kennedy

I offer abundant thanks to Spirit, and my Bright Ones- for their guidance on this journey. As I explained in the Introduction, these Magical Inner Journeys come through me rather than from me, and I am grateful for each and every image and word that flows through me to the page.

My appreciation goes out to my 7th grade Physical Education teacher for that very first inner journey back in 1969. Also to Ruby Dillard, the principal of Amelia County Elementary School where I was lucky enough to teach from 1978-1984. She always championed my creativity and imagination, and encouraged me to share these gifts with my second graders.

Alan Cohen's guided imageries and teaching have inspired much of my own inner work since 1987. I would be a very different person if I had not stumbled across that cassette tape of his meditations during my first dark night of the soul.

I can't express enough gratitude for the influence that my therapist, Fran Booth, had on me during the years after my first cancer journey. Her kindness, compassion, and wise insight gently guided me forward and away from that difficult diagnosis, and steered me towards a fuller, happier life. Fran worked with me with the Internal Family Systems model, and the imagery in my inner world that we explored had a tremendous impact on my journey.

I am ever and always grateful to Seena Frost for giving us the gift of SoulCollage®. My life has been transformed because of her, many times over, and in all ways affirmative.

Kylea Taylor, President of SoulCollage Inc., offered excellent suggestions so that I could bring this book to completion. I am also thankful for her compassionate mentoring of me as a Facilitator Trainer over the years.

Carol Coogan is an unrivaled goddess of creativity and book design. I am so grateful for the enthusiasm, expertise, and magical beauty that she brought to this project, including the amazing cover.

Marti Beddoe and Cheryl Finley are true companions who encourage and nurture me both personally and professionally. Marti and Cheryl are the sisters I never had; their presence in my life gifts me with a wellspring of peace and joy. I am grateful every day for the irrefutable fact of their friendship.

I also would like to shower buckets of love and appreciation onto every SoulCollager who attended one or more of my workshops, classes, retreats, or Trainings over the years. Because of you, I have become a better Facilitator. Because of your responses to these guided imageries, I have been inspired to open myself up to more and more of these Magical Inner Journeys.

My husband Jeff deserves mention here for his unwavering support and encouragement as I continue to bring SoulCollage® out into the world through my books, workshops, retreats, online teachings, and Facilitator Trainings. Several times a year, he carries (to and from the car) all of the heavy bins and boxes of magazines, mat boards, images, and other paraphernalia that accompany me to my workshops and retreats. With his strength, he also carries my heart, and I am grateful for the 27 years of love and laughter we have shared.

Resources

Books About SoulCollage®

SoulCollage® Evolving, by Seena B. Frost. *An Intuitive Collage Process for Self-Discovery and Community.*

The Ethics of Caring, by Kylea Taylor. *Finding Right Relationship with Clients.*

Through the Eyes of SoulCollage®, by Anne Marie Bennett. *Reflections on Life Via the SoulCollage® Lens.*

Into the Heart of SoulCollage®, by Anne Marie Bennett. *Diving Into the Many Gifts and Possibilities of SoulCollage®.*

Books About Guided Imagery

Guided Imagery Meditation: *The Artistry of Words,* by Sarah Mendenhall-Luhmer

Guided Meditations, Explorations and Healings, by Stephen Levine

Imagery In You: *Mining for Treasure in Your Inner World,* by Jenny Garrison

Inner Journeys: *Meditations and Visualizations,* by Gloria Chadwick

Laughter, Tears, Silence: *Expressive Meditations to Calm Your Mind and Open Your Heart,* by Pragito Dove

The Joy of Visualization: *75 Creative Ways to Enhance Your Life,* by Valerie Wells

Seeds of Light: *Healing Meditations for Body and Soul,* by Elizabeth K. Stratton

Music

Sometimes it's good to guide these Magical Inner Journeys with just the power of your voice, but other times you might want to have soothing music playing in the background. Here are some recordings that I like to use. They are especially good because there is no discernible melody at any time. Recognizable melodies tend to distract people from the inner journey.

As always, try these out before using with a group. Practice reading your chosen script aloud with the music in the background, then notice how it sounds . . . and especially how it feels. If it doesn't feel good to you, *don't use it!*

Dream: A Liquid Mind Experience, by Liquid Mind *(anything by Liquid Mind is good!)*

Healing Spirit, by Diane Arkenstone

Return of the Angels, by Philip Chapman

Spiritual Healing, by Deuter *(anything by Deuter is good!)*

Meditative Mind- This is a YouTube channel with soothing music using Solfreggio frequencies.

Websites

SoulCollage.com: Visit this site to find out more about SoulCollage®, and Seena Frost who created the process. There is also information here about how to become a SoulCollage® Facilitator, along with books, CDs, and supplies for your own SoulCollage® journey.

KaleidoSoul.com: KaleidoSoul is dedicated to the art and practice of SoulCollage®. It is your SoulCollage® playground! There are pages here on every aspect of the process- from card making, to journaling with your cards, to doing focused card readings . . . and everything in between! We offer online courses for beginners as well as those who've been doing SoulCollage® for a while. You'll also find MP3 recordings and CDs of many of the Magical Inner Journeys scripts in this book on these pages: KaleidoSoul.com/cds and KaleidoSoul.com/oasis

Your brain is wider than the sky.

~ Emily Dickinson

Printed in Poland
by Amazon Fulfillment
Poland Sp. z o.o., Wrocław